Bounce

A memoir of resilience

By Susan McCorkindale

ALSO BY SUSAN MCCORKINDALE

Confessions of a Counterfeit Farm Girl

500 Acres and No Place to Hide, More Confessions of a Counterfeit Farm Girl

For my mother, Joan Costantino.

Contents

PROLOGUE

Part One

LIFE AFTER DEATH

Ashes, Ashes, We All Wore Dad

Cancer's Trophy is Toast

Got Pain? You've Come to the Wrong Place

All Decisions Made by the Management Are Final
(Even if They're Not Popular)

Not the Usual Routine

So Much for Self-diagnosis

Death's Not Up for Discussion

Part Two

**WHAT TO EXPECT
WHEN YOU NEVER EXPECTED TO BE A WIDOW**

When Good Moms Go Dad

Wine. It's What's for Breakfast

Little Gold Anchors. Away

At Least I Know I'm Not Crazy

Hell if I Know

Mommy/Daddy Houses Need Not Apply

How Better to Hide the Blood?

A Question of Cancer

Farm (Mis)Management 101

The Worst Mom in the History of Motherhood

Too Much Time on My Hands. And Face

Taking My Lumps

The D-word

No "Family Guy" at Grandma's

Who Knew My Kid Could Read So Much into a Cookie?

The Winemaker

Part Three

THE END, AND THE BEGINNING

When Mother Nature says, "Now!"

P.T.E.D.
(Post Traumatic Ex-husband Disorder)

And Then She Came Along

Oh Please. "You Look So Healthy!" is

Totally Code for "Girlfriend, You're Getting Fat!"

My Apartment is Lemonade

You Can Quote Me on That

Grateful for the New Day
(No Matter How Uncertain a Day It Is)

The Bamboo Rescuer

Losing Wendy

Getting Through It

Put It Out There

Be the Person You'd Want to Be Quarantined With

Just Another Blue-gened Girl

There's a Bear by the Pool

EPILOGUE

***

Resilience is My Superpower
31 resilience-building meditations. One for every day of the month.

Author's Note

My sons' names are Casey and Cuyler, pronounced Kyler. My late husband selected Casey in honor of legendary New York Yankees manager, Casey Stengel, and Cuyler, in honor of Hazen "KiKi" Cuyler who hit the winning home run for the Pittsburgh Pirates in the 1925 World Series. Obviously, he was a big baseball fan. I just wanted two names that started with C.

"Life is not about how fast you run, or how high you climb,

but how well you bounce."

— Vivian Komari

Prologue

I'm sitting at lunch with my friend, Laura, who's very, very, carefully giving me her thoughts on the very first draft of this book, all of which I'm writing on the back of my credit card statement because, despite all my years of being a writer, I still always forget to pack a notepad. I don't usually carry my credit card bill around, but later I need to share it with my boyfriend who's helping me pay down the balance. Obviously, the life of a non-notepad-carrying writer is not very lucrative, and I wonder if I started carrying one if things would change. They wouldn't; I write for no other reason than because I can't help myself and because I've always believed my experiences and feelings are universal and if someone reads my words and sees it's not just them going through whatever they're going through and finds hope in what I share, that's enough for me. That's my compensation. Though a little more money would be nice.

Poor Laura. She's pushed aside her salad and is maybe on sentence two or three of her uber-hesitant constructive criticism and I can't take it anymore. She read the draft two weeks ago and between her schedule and mine, it was tough finding a time to get together. I'm a little antsy to hear what she has to say, but I can deal with her telling me that it's awful. I can deal with her telling me to scrap the whole thing. What I can't deal with is my beautiful friend, who probably weighs eleven pounds soaking wet, not eating her lunch.

"Laura," I say, reaching across the table for her hand, "it's alright. I have very thick skin. Wrinkled, but thick. I can take whatever you've got to say, but I can't take you not eating your rabbit food."

"I'll eat it," she says, tapping the top of the plastic to-go container, "though I probably shouldn't. I've put on weight."

"I thought you looked a little too healthy."

"Wise ass," she laughs.

I love Laura and admire her tremendously. She's crazy smart, completely clueless as to how pretty she is, and has a voice like Kathleen Turner. I, on the other hand, still possess the New Jersey regionalism I arrived in Virginia with fifteen years ago despite myriad attempts to eradicate it. There are times it's less pronounced, but just one phone call to my mom and it's back full bore.

"Girlfriend," I say, "I've been waiting two weeks to see you. Tell me to start over. Tell me to scrap the whole thing. I don't care, ok I do, but tell me something."

"You cannot scrap it," she says, shaking her head and looking me straight in the eye. "You have to finish it."

"Ok. So….?"

She takes a huge breath. I let go of her hand, my pen and credit card statement at the ready, and a woman stops to tell Laura how much her dogs adore the pet food she recommended. Of course, they do, I think. We're lunching at Gentle Harvest, a part café, part super high-end grocery store renowned for stocking only organic, locally produced, mouthwatering everything and Laura, a passionate animal lover and a lifelong vegan to prove it, oversees its pet food division. My guess is whatever this lady's dogs have been enjoying for dinner is far healthier than anything I've ever put in my own body and they have Laura to thank for it.

"Saved by the bell," I tease as the woman walks away. "Spill it, sister."

"Ok," she replies, as we simultaneously lean in toward each other. "You need to tell people, readers, right up front that this book isn't just about a woman who loses the man she loves to cancer. This is about a woman who's left in the middle of basically nowhere, with one son who has autism and another who has the world at his feet but who's so undone at his dad's death that his anxiety threatens to steal his future before it starts."

I nod.

"You need to tell them that this is about so much more than a city girl who becomes a farm manager—"

"You mean mis-manager," I laugh.

"No, I don't. Just listen," she continues, and I'm taken back by the tears in her eyes. "You handled 500-acres, two kids, and three dogs. You went back to work. You pushed Casey to the brink of hating you to help him do things those stupid doctors said he'd never do. How did you do that?"

"Do what? Push Casey?"

"All of it."

"You'd have handled things the same way."

"I'm not sure I would have, and I know lots of people who definitely wouldn't have."

She pauses and I realize two things: how much my dear friend loves me, and how easy it would have been to go down the grief rabbit hole so many give into. But I couldn't. My kids lost one parent. There was no way they were losing two.

"And then, then you fell in love. We were all so happy for you. He seemed like a great guy. Good to you and your boys; who could ask for more? Sadly, he turned out to be—"

"An asshole!" we say at the same time.

"What was it, like, a whole month after you got married that it went to hell? And you didn't leave."

"I was an idiot," I reply.

"No, you're not an idiot. You tried to save one husband from his disease, why wouldn't you try to save another? You loved him. Even after you left him, you loved him. You mourned that divorce like a death."

"It was a death."

"Do you know how many people would have curled up under their desk and stayed there, Susan? You didn't though. You came right back. Launched a successful magazine. Built a speaking career. And your sons! Stu would be so proud."

"They are pretty awesome."

"People need to know that this is the journey you're about to take them on. They need a little head's up." And then she laughs. "Guess it might have been nice if you'd had one, too, huh?"

"I don't know," I reply. "I might not have made the trip."

"But you did, and there are people out there going through similar things or who will at some point be faced with a similar situation. They'll lose someone they love, get divorced, lose their job, face financial ruin, you name it, and they need to hear how you kept going. How you just kept bouncing back." She takes a last sip of her lemonade and collects the salad she hasn't touched.

"You're going to eat that, right?" I ask.

"Taking it to my desk now," she replies.

We stand and hug, barely escaping being trampled by a couple who've been eying our table. Laura sends her love to my boyfriend, Robert, the saint who's helping me with my credit card, and I send mine to her husband, Larry. I'm turning away when she touches the sleeve of my sweater.

"You have to finish it, Susan. Promise me you'll finish it and that you'll give people a little head's up at the beginning, so they know to buckle up."

We laugh and I promise her I will.

And so, I have.

And here we go.

Part One
Life After Death

"In three words I can sum up everything I've learned about life: it goes on."

Robert Frost

Ashes, Ashes, We All Wore Dad
(And Pete! Why Does Everyone Keep Forgetting Pete?)

"Mom, wait! We have to do Pete's ashes, too!" shouted Cuyler as he ran back into the house. It was a Sunday morning in the still chilly spring and he, Casey, and I were heading out to spread Stu's ashes on the farm.

"What?" I replied, practically falling down the front steps which really would've been bad as I was holding the open urn. "You want to mix the dog's ashes with Dad's?"

He stopped and looked at me. "You said we could!"

I say a lot of things. Things like, "Clean your room" and "Bring in the mail" and "The next time one of you spends thirty-bucks on iTunes, I'm closing the account," but nobody listens and if they do? They forget as soon as they've sworn up and down it won't happen again.

I was counting on Cuy to forget I'd said this, too. But he didn't, so Casey and I stood there in the thin yellow sunshine and the cool breeze, waiting.

"Can I hold it?" Casey asked, referring to the urn.

I craned my head back to look my super tall, skinny as a rail first born in his baby blues. "You won't drop it, right?"

"You mean like you nearly did?" He rolled his eyes. "No."

"Good, because if you do? Dad will go everywhere, and you know how he hated to travel."

We both laughed because it was true. My husband was a homebody whose idea of a getaway was going to the Tractor Supply five minutes from the farm. We did convince him to go to Myrtle Beach a few times but while the three of us enjoyed the sun, surf, and nightly trips to the boardwalk for dinner, shopping, and the chance to ride a mechanical bull with the rest of the masses, the poor guy didn't relax until he saw the "Mosby Heritage Area" signs on the return trip.

"They're not in the den," said Cuy poking his head out the door. "Where did you put them?"

"In the basement—" I stopped at the look of horror that crossed my kid's face. "What?"

"How could you put Pete in the basement? You always hated him!"

"I didn't hate Pete," I shouted as Cuy turned and ran down the hall. "I hated how he smelled!"

Honestly, when that dog started sweating, he let off an odor that made your eyes water. He died a few days after Stu and the three of us think he went to keep him company in Heaven where, hopefully, he smells like a rose and not one of our 350-head of cattle on a ninety-degree day.

"The urn," Casey said, taking it from me as Cuy reappeared on the porch carrying Pete's ashes.

"Mom!" he cried. "You put him next to old paint cans! How could you?"

I replied that I was sorry, and that I thought Pete would be cooler in the basement, but Cuy wasn't buying it. Tears crept from the corners of his eyes as he clutched the dog's little oak coffin to his New York Giants tee shirt. "You wanted me to forget to bring him today, didn't you?"

"No, no, I didn't," I lied. "Ok, maybe a little. I'm sorry. It was wrong of me."

"Mom," Casey said, "the wind's picking up. We need to do this before we make a mess of Dad's ashes."

"And Pete!" cried Cuy. "Why does everyone keep forgetting Pete?"

We'd decided we would spread ashes first on Stu's fruit trees, so I lead the way down to them. He'd planted one peach, one pear and two apple trees a year or two before he got sick. He'd read books on them, cared for them, watered them until we both worried our well would run dry, but they never produced a single decent piece of fruit, or at least not any the kids or I would eat. He would walk into the house, munching a mutant peach, his pockets stuffed with more mutant peaches, roll them like little rocks onto the kitchen table and say, "Susan A., these aren't bad! Have a bite!" and the kids and I would run for cover. One bout of diarrhea I could handle. Four was not my idea of fun. Now, one of the trees was dead, the other three weren't far behind, and the ground was covered in ancient pieces of rotted fruit.

A sob caught in Cuy's throat. "I hate looking at this shit," he whispered.

"Dad loved these trees," said Casey.

"Yeah well they're dead. And he's dead—"

"And Pete's dead," I interjected, trying to let my younger son know I would not forget his beloved pet ever again. "But today is about remembering them alive and spreading their ashes over the places that meant the most to them."

I looked from one son to the other and for the first time since Stu got sick, I saw them, really saw them. For sure they were taller and broader than they'd been two years earlier, but now I saw the exhaustion in their eyes. Fear, too. The guy who'd been in charge of this place was gone and for my first official at bat, I'd chosen to take them on a tour of everything he loved that died while he was dying.

My kids had every right to be afraid. Clearly, I had no idea what I was doing.

"Gentlemen," I said, summoning every ounce of fake it 'til you make it I could muster, "Casey is right. Dad loved these trees, and Pete loved being with Dad no matter what he was doing so, in a way, he loved them too."

"Probably just to pee on," Cuy offered.

"Not just that," Casey said, his eyes scouring the ground.

"Excellent!" I said. "We've discovered that Pete's role was to provide fertilizer. How about we honor his efforts and, more importantly dad's, by spreading some ashes?"

So, we did. Or at least we tried to. What no one tells you about spreading ashes is that they don't go where you want them to go. Over the course of four dead and dying fruit trees, with the sun paling by the moment and the wind steadily picking up steam, we did our best to toss handfuls of chalky grey ash onto the ground only to have it whip right back at us and into our eyes and mouths, cover our faces, and coat our clothes.

And then, looking like three sooty chimney sweeps, we proceeded to what was once Stu's thriving vegetable and flower garden, an enormous patch of land he spent hours tending and upon which he grew tomatoes, cucumbers, pumpkins that occasionally came in ahead of season (July to be exact), and the freshest, juiciest lettuce I've ever tasted and will never taste again.

The boys didn't get any further than the gate.

"I can't go in there, mom," said Casey, looking from the overturned wheel barrel to the piles of unopened, weather-beaten bags of fertilizer, to the rusted clippers and trowel on the ground beside them.

"I'll keep him company," said Cuyler, looking at me.

I couldn't blame them.

I took Stu's urn, said I'd be back for Pete's, and went through the gate. I walked up and down the dust- and weed-choked rows slowly, spreading my dead husband's ashes on the dream of living off the land that had died with him.

I don't know what other people say when they honor their loved ones in this way, but all I could say as I took in his withered strawberry bushes, toppled tomato cages that clung to each other in a heap like frightened orphans, and the gnarled vines of the pumpkins we'd laughed so hard over as we decorated dozens one summer, was I'm sorry.

I'm sorry you got sick. I'm sorry I couldn't save you. I'm sorry I couldn't keep the things you loved alive. I'm sorry, sweetheart. I'm so sorry.

And I'm really sorry I can't make these stupid ashes stay put.

Now the wind was making even the dead plants dance and because my tears and the ashes clinging to my contact lenses had formed a nice paste, I was practically blind. *What in God's name is the protocol here?* I wondered. Take half of Stu and a good chunk of Pete back into the house and try again tomorrow? Or keep going and end up wearing more ashes than we spread, in which case my poor husband and his stinky pup were most definitely going into the house and directly into the washing machine.

I stood there frozen with indecision and freezing because the sun had decided to call it a day. *Are you trying to tell me something, Stu?* I thought, looking up at the sky. *What do I do?* I begged.

He'd called all the shots, made all the decisions. It was he who decided in the late summer of 2004 that we should take a six-hour ride from our home in suburban New Jersey to look at a 500-acre beef cattle farm in Northern Virginia. Sure, we'd talked about fleeing what we called the tri-state target zone since September 11th, but I always thought that meant we'd move to another suburb. You know, someplace with sidewalks and people and regular pets like dogs and cats, and not to a veritable petting zoo. But the petting zoo, which shortly after our arrival the following January grew to include goats, chickens, polo ponies, and the occasional Clydesdales, in addition to the cows, won out. Stu wanted to farm, I wanted him to be happy, and we both wanted Casey and Cuyler to grow up someplace safe. So farmers we became. Or, more accurately, he became.

I, on the other hand, became a fish out of water. A former magazine marketing pro and city girl with absolutely zero hankering to be a farm hand, I took to my laptop and launched a blog called *Confessions of a Counterfeit Farm Girl*. Once a week, I wrote about my latest mishap with the hens, misguided attempt to corral cattle, and misplaced enthusiasm for waterfowl.

Stu thought the fact that he farmed, and I wrote farm funnies was hysterical. And when, much to our surprise, I was invited to turn my blog into a book, no one was prouder for me than he was.

Three years after our move to cow country, the book came out and we celebrated like any family of four enjoying fifteen minutes of fame: we went to Disney World. It was an indescribably happy time. And then it happened.

The following fall, Stu was diagnosed with pancreatic cancer. Take no prisoners types that we both are, we decided we'd beat it. He started chemo, I started my second memoir, and together we started the boys and ourselves on a strict diet of situation comedies, funny movies, and every word Dave Barry's ever written (with a little Nora Ephron thrown in just for me). Laughter, and the

Lombardi Comprehensive Cancer Center at Georgetown University Hospital, was our best medicine. And it worked until it didn't.

Twenty-one months after his diagnosis, he died. Just a few short months after that, my second book, *500 Acres and No Place to Hide: More Confessions of a Counterfeit Farm Girl* was published. Part of me felt badly that my number one fan wasn't here to see it, but another part knows without a doubt that he did. The proof is in the reviews the book received, and the fact that the following February the New York Giants beat the New England Patriots in the Super Bowl. Again.

If it had been him holding my urn – well, first of all he'd be sprinkling me all along the Jersey shore and, surreptitiously of course, in the size seven clearance section at DSW – he'd have known what to do. And even if he didn't know what to do, he'd have done something other than stand there.

I missed him so much in that moment, I started to cry. Again. Harder than before. So hard that miraculously, my contacts cleared. *Whew*, I thought. *At least now I can see.*

And then my left lens popped out of my eye. This was going about as well as Stu's memorial service. (A tale I shall share shortly, I promise.)

My left eye closed and still clutching the urn, I walked back to the boys.

"You ok?" Casey asked. "What's wrong with your eye?"

"I lost a lens." I replied.

"You're wearing an awful lot of Dad," Cuy said.

"And you're not wearing enough," I replied, gesturing like I might toss a handful at him.

"God mom, no!" Casey cried. "We'll all go to hell!"

What makes you think we're not there now? I thought. I turned to Cuy and looked at Pete's urn. "I can't go back in there, sweetheart."

"I wasn't going to let you," he replied.

The three of us stood there for a moment, cold and heartbroken and blind. Well, I was blind.

"You want to go in the house?" I asked. "Finish tomorrow?"

"Oh, hell no," spat Cuy. "I'm not dragging this out another day."

Case reached for Stu's urn. "Let's just get this over with ok?"

I nodded, and we turned toward the chicken coop, the last stop on our spread Dad's ashes (and Pete's, don't forget Pete!) on the places he treasured tour.

The silence is what I remember most about the coop that morning. What was once a place filled with life and smells and sounds – Stu's beloved rooster Hef, so named for Hugh Hefner, doing his thing at the crack of dawn, two dozen chickens cackling, pecking the ground and sometimes each other, all three dogs – Grundy, Tug and Pete – trying to play with them (which always resulted in Stu scolding the dogs, trying to shoo them away, and ultimately shouting, "Susan A.! Can you *please* put these hounds in the house?") – was now absolutely still. Scratch and feed beaten by the weather into clumps covered the ground. Watering tins toppled and dented and red with rust lay in a forest of weeds, and the three concrete steps, now chipped and tilted, led to a latched door straining at its loosened hinges.

"It looks like a crime scene," said Cuy.

"All we need is yellow tape and a chalk outline of a dead chicken," said Casey.

The three of us lost it laughing. *Stu, I thought, we've done it. We've passed our sick sense of humor onto the kids. Congratulations to us!* My husband loved a good, quick comeback and would have been fist bumping and high fiving Case for having come up with one. Plus, it gave us a final boost to finish what we started.

Carefully as they could, my sons spread the last of the ashes around the coop. It will come as no surprise that the wind didn't cooperate, and we wore a lot more than we'd have liked, but still, the majority of Stu's ashes went where we knew he would want to be. More than the fruit trees or the garden, he loved his "girls." And someday, when the coop once again finds itself full of chickens, he'll be there to help protect them.

Pete too, of course.

Cancer's Trophy is Toast

I've read about people who, even years after their spouse's death, cannot bring themselves to do anything with their loved ones' clothes. For some, leaving a scarf on a hook in the mudroom where a late wife last hung it brings them comfort. For others, leaving shoes in the doorway where a late husband last kicked them off makes them feel a little more like he might return, slip them on, and go out to garden. Sweet, isn't it?

I'm not that sweet.

As far as I'm concerned, scarves belong in the coat closet, and shoes belong in the clothes closet. For weeks after my husband's death, I walked around gathering things and mumbling "a place for everything, and everything in its place."

Hold on. That's not exactly accurate.

I didn't walk around mumbling. I raced around mumbling and all too frequently shouting, "Dammit, Stu! Who leaves socks on a bookshelf? Thank you for giving me one more thing to pick up. One more thing for me to take care of. You're so selfish!"

And then I'd cry, apologize to my dead husband, and berate myself for not handling things the way some other, better, wife – correction, widow – would.

I was exhausted, but I couldn't stop moving. Every day was a mad dash of cleaning the kitchen, sweeping the dog hair off the stairs, doing load after load of laundry, and finding another item of my late husband's clothing in some far-flung location on the farm. Looking back at that wretchedly wet, dogs-covered-in-mud-and-stinking-like-bad-fish spring, I can see that perpetual motion was my way of keeping grief and fear at bay. Only I didn't think that, then. I thought, *I'm just cleaning up. My husband was sick for two years. I need to get things back in order, focus on my sons, make sure their sheets and clothes are clean, that there's food in the fridge and flowers on the table.*

Seriously Susan?

Food, yes, but when did your kids ever care about clean clothes? You practically pay them to part with the shorts they've been wearing since departing for a sleepover on Friday and returning on Tuesday. And flowers? Girlfriend, you need a nap.

But I couldn't, wouldn't, nap. If I sat for just a moment to admire the tulips I cut from the hundreds Stu planted for me around our sweet, four-square Colonial farmhouse we dubbed "Nate's Place" the very first time we laid eyes on it, placed squarely on the beautiful butcherblock table in our bright yellow kitchen bedecked with rooster plates and signs that read, "Tonight's Dinner Options: 1. Take it. 2. Leave it," and "We interrupt this family for football season," panic would see the pause in my momentum as an invitation to wrap its long, skinny fingers around my neck and squeeze, rendering me unable to breathe and giving free reign to the thoughts I ran from all day, every day.

The kids are scared. I'm scared. The kids are scared. I'm scared. The kids are scared. I am really scared. And I am really, really, angry.

Nope. There'd be no napping for this new widow. Just more pissed off cleaning, cleaning out, cursing my dead husband, and then apologizing to him. Which brings me back to the folks who can't part with their loved one's belongings.

Up until this point I'd been washing and setting aside every item of Stu's clothing I found in his workshop, the equipment shed, and the barn. Before he got sick, he'd go out to work dressed in layers, peel them off during the day, and leave jackets, long-sleeve tee shirts, short-sleeve tee shirts, flannel shirts, denim shirts, hats, and gloves wherever he was when he decided he was too warm to continue wearing them. Days, more often weeks, later he'd demand to know what had become of his blue Budweiser tee shirt or Ridgewood Junior Football cap and accuse me of throwing them out. Now both of those items, indeed much of my husband's beloved attire, deserved a decent Christian burial. They weren't on their last legs. They hadn't had legs since Jesus invented Jesus sandals. But throw them out? Are you crazy? Hell hath no fury like a McCorkindale man who can't find his favorite Jackson Browne concert tee from The Pretender tour in 1976.

To be clear, every item I found had been lying wherever I found it, since the summer of 2009. You can't imagine the layers of bird poop, mud, chicken scratch, and crushed range cubes it was covered in.

His closet, which held all his dressy stuff – nice pants, nice shirts, sweaters, dress shoes, you know what I mean – hadn't been touched since that time, either. From the moment he got sick until the moment he died twenty-two months later he wore none of it. Thanks to the blazing ineptitude of his original healthcare team, he lost sixty pounds between July and September of that year. By the time I got him to real doctors and a real diagnosis, nothing in his closet fit. He never opened it again, and neither did I.

Cleaning it out was awful. I opened the doors and the dust raced at me like kids fleeing school for summer break. It stung my eyes and stuck to my face which, believe it or not, made me feel good, really good, in a sort of "Take that, you bastards!" way. I even recall thinking, *The joke's on you, dust kiddies. You're stuck to my tears and clearly not joining the rest of your crew at the beach or pool or wherever dust particles prefer to vacation.*

And yes, I laughed.

Every pair of dressy pants, every button-down shirt, his good shoes, sneakers, flip flops, handkerchiefs, belts, and ties, were totally covered in dust. Sure, the ties were probably like that before he got sick because he didn't wear them, but at least that was his decision. As for the rest of his things, particularly his pants, covered along the creases in mini mountain formations of dust coated so thick I had to pick them off, that was cancer's call.

Cancer sucks.

Stu's closet sucked.

There it stood, a shrine to where the buck stopped. To where his life stopped. Ground zero. One day he needed what was in it, the next he never touched it again. One day he didn't have cancer, the next he did. The dust choked clothing was proof, as if I needed more, that despite almost two years of trying, the tumor had emerged triumphant. The closet was its trophy.

Ain't no way any of that stuff was staying in my house.

Pants, shirts, the hangers they hung on, shoes, belts, and ties (save one, a Nicole Miller baseball themed tie Casey always loved) went into plastic bags faster than my sons can plow through a package of Chips Ahoy. The bags went into the back of our Durango even faster. Then I hightailed it down to the thrift store.

I arrived, and the lovely, older African American man who works there greeted me with his usual smile and "Need some help?" query as he approached the car. I popped the hatch and grabbed a bag. I never need help, plus I'm always worried he's exhausted from being on his feet all day. Yes, I bring things to the thrift store that frequently. It's just how I am.

I despise clutter, both the kind I can see, piled on countertops and tables, and the kind stuffed into closets, drawers, and Rubbermaid totes stacked in the basement. It's this kind of clutter, the hidden crap of questionable wedding presents, holiday-themed napkins and paper plates bought on sale for "next year" and promptly forgotten, Precious Moments figurines I received as gifts but never displayed because frankly, they frighten me, tablecloths I bought, hated, and forgot to return, unused picture frames, candlestick holders, placemats, linen napkins that require ironing (ironing!), that taunts me from wherever I've stuffed it. Like the telltale heart, I can hear it mocking my "no clutter" motto as loud and clear as my kids announcing, "We're out of ice cream!"

This kind of clutter may be out of sight, but it's never out of my mind until it's out of my house.

Thus, my concern for the nice man at the thrift store.

Anyway, I thanked him for his offer, said I only had a few bags, that they weren't heavy, and I'd be out of his hair in no time. While I unloaded, we made small talk. About the weather, his back (see? My concern is far from unfounded!), and how busy he'd been that afternoon. Then he asked, did I want a receipt to claim the donation on my taxes? "No," I said. (I mean, why bother? Cancer had already claimed it.), and how was I going to spend the rest of the lovely day?

For some reason I responded with "I'm going to Home Depot." So that's what I did. I bought Clorox spray, plastic gloves, and the biggest bundle of paper towels I could find.

Then I went home and scrubbed the closet to within an inch of its life. I scrubbed the walls and the shelves and the rods where Stu's clothes once hung. I vacuumed. Then I scrubbed again – harder, faster, angrier than before. What I wanted was to rip the whole damn thing out. Standing inside of it felt like I was standing inside a cancer cell. Crazier still was my sense that the cancer was taunting me. *I was here,* it hissed, *and I WON. This closet is MINE.*

No, I thought. You've taken enough from us. You're out. I'm getting rid of you. But how?

And then, suddenly, I recalled what people do to refresh a room when it's been used by a smoker.

They paint.

Not an apples-to-apples comparison, but still.

So, paint I did. Over the next 48 hours, I attacked the closet, putting three coats of white paint on the walls and shelves. Pure, bright white. The first coat went on like a fistfight, my brush hitting the wall like a punching bag. When I was done, I looked like something in a snow globe; specks of white paint dotted my hair and face, my eyelashes and bottom lip. And forget my clothes. They were covered (and clearly not destined for the thrift shop). I looked pretty funny, but I felt great. Susan 1, cancer-riddled closet, 0.

Several hours later, still high from my big win, I applied the second coat. I used a roller this time, going up and down the walls, each stroke a barrier between cancer and the closet. Between cancer and us. I hit the corners with these small sponge brushes my dad taught me to use one Christmas Eve when he decided to paint the living room mere hours before Santa – and fourteen family members – were due to arrive, and I dabbed at the seams, nooks, and crannies again and again, until they were thick with paint, and there wasn't a single crack cancer could use to creep back in.

For the first time since the fall of Stu's diagnosis, I didn't need an Ambien to sleep that night. I fell into my bed and was out before my uniquely highlighted hair touched my pillow.

By mid-afternoon the next day, the closet was dry. It didn't need a third coat, but I had it in my head that, for safety's sake, it was getting one. Carefully and calmly this time, I rolled and brushed and dabbed. And when it was done and gleaming, I stepped back and smiled.

Cancer's trophy was toast.

Bounce Boost

People often ask me how I can laugh and find the humor in things like cancer and caregiving, death, and raising a child with Autism, and the answer is really pretty simple: laughter gives me distance; it buys me a moment to step back from the situation, get a grip, and get on with it. There are those who would call my response a defense mechanism, and maybe it is, but there's nothing wrong with defending yourself when necessary and, when dealing with a situation that's hopeless, laughter – and the momentary distance it provides – is the equivalent of putting your oxygen mask on first, and then helping someone else with theirs.

I was crying when I opened Stu's closet. I knew I'd find his beautiful sweaters, beloved Marine Corps belt buckle, and the cleats he wore to coach Cuyler's junior football team covered in grit. But when that dust raced out with such glee, as if my sole purpose in opening the door was to free it, and hundreds of happy particles met their fate on my face? It struck me as funny. One moment these nasty, cancer-caused flecks thought they'd fly off to live happily ever after, and the next I was scrubbing them away, certain I could hear cries of, "No, please, no! We've just spent two years trapped in a closet! Have mercy!" as they disappeared down the drain.

As Roger Rabbit said, "Sometimes a laugh is the only weapon we have."

Why not wield it?

**Got pain?
You've come to the wrong place**

Like the closet it claimed, cancer took one of the cabinets in the kitchen, too. Unlike the closet though, I didn't want to rip the cabinet out of the wall and burn it in the backyard. I just wanted to boil it, or have it exorcised or something.

Why? Because it housed what we referred to as the McPharmacy: all three of its shelves were filled to bursting with Stu's pain medications.

I referred to the top shelf as the shit shelf, as in "This stuff doesn't do shit." It didn't matter that I couldn't reach it without a stepladder or an assist from my older son Casey, who's 6'5". I'd just whip the bottle of whatever pills did nothing to ease Stu's pain up there, curse the prescription's ineptitude and the precious time it cost us, and search the bottom shelf as fast as possible for a substitute.

If I may digress for just a moment for those who might be wondering what I mean about the prescription costing us time, it's simply this: there's nothing worse than chasing pain. In fact, rule #1 of cancer caregiving is Stay Ahead of the Pain. If the doctor or the pharmacist or the label on the bottle says, "Take 1 every four hours" and your patient's taken it at two o'clock, you're on the road to disaster – and maybe the emergency room – if you wait until six to give him or her another dose. Five-thirty is good, and, in my experience, five-fifteen is better.

Right below the shit shelf was the "probably shit, but let's give it another shot" shelf. This held all the pills with "extenuating circumstances." Medications that worked only once, but didn't deserve the shit shelf yet because maybe they'd work another time, others that made my husband sick, but maybe it was because he ate before he took them or he didn't eat before he took them or he didn't take them with enough water or, or, or. And finally, there were those that sometimes worked but only if I paired them with others that sometimes worked. The "probably shit, but let's give it another shot" shelf wasn't ideal, but having it was a lifesaver on more than one occasion.

And finally, there was the bottom shelf. The one I could reach, the one that held the meds that were working at the moment. Sometimes there were two bottles in it. Other times there were three, and a box of pain patches. Unlike the "shit" and "probably shit" shelves, it was so empty you could hear your voice echo if you screamed into it. I never did that, by the way. When I needed to scream, I went outside and gave our rooster a run for his money.

Unlike the closet, which was upstairs and out of sight, the cabinet taunted me from the moment I turned my coffee on in the morning. Gritty and sticky with failure and fear, dashed hopes and unanswered prayers, it represented every avenue we'd put our faith in, just to find we'd reached another dead end.

I cleaned it out the morning after Stu's death. My mom was there. Two weeks prior, I found her standing on our front porch, a Manassas taxicab driving off down our gravel road.

"Mom!" I cried hugging her, relief and joy and gratitude and more relief flooding every bone in my exhausted body. "What are you doing here?" To which she replied, "Sue, please don't be mad. I know you have everything under control. But maybe you need a nap?"

I have never been so happy to see anyone in my life.

So, she was there as I pulled every vial, box, and bottle off the shelves and attacked them with Clorox spray and paper towels. She held the step stool so I could get everything off the "shit" shelf and scrub it. And then she watched as I flushed what was probably two grand (if I sold it on the street) worth of Oxycodone and Oxycontin down the toilet.

I opened each of the little vials, poured, and flushed, saying, "Thanks for nothing" and "You did shit" as we watched the tiny orbs spin away.

Cancer is so physically painful, and pancreatic cancer hurts like something only bastards like Hitler or Timothy McVeigh should have to endure. The Oxy, the Dilaudid, the Fentanyl, did nothing. My hatred for those "painkillers" is almost as great as my hatred for Stu's cancer. They gave him such little relief that, by the end, I was pumping him full of the stuff. I couldn't just sit there and hold his hand and try to distract him from the pain wracking his body. It was bad enough I had a baby monitor set up so I could hear him all over the house. Was I supposed to put up a brightly colored mobile too?

He wasn't a baby. He was a man. A good man. And he was suffering.

"You know, mom," I said, "Hitler and Timothy McVeigh got off easy. How in God's name does God let that happen?"

She shook her head and started putting coffee cups that had been stuffed into another cabinet on the bottom shelf of the former McPharmacy.

"Oh God, no, mom," I said. "I don't want to use it. I hate that cabinet."

"Why?" she asked, whipping around and gesturing at me with the bird bath-size Bucknell University mug Stu's goddaughter sent him when she was an undergrad.

"Did the shelves collapse?" She asked.

I shook my head no.

"Did the door fall off?"

Again, no.

"Did even one of its hinges come loose in all the time you needed it?"

"No, but—"

"You should be grateful for this cabinet, Sue. It did its job, even if its contents didn't." Then she turned, placed the Bucknell mug on the bottom shelf, and I burst out laughing.

"What?" she said.

"Can you imagine if the door had come off its hinges?" I said.

"You bet I can," she replied. "You'd have been stuck looking at three shelves worth of clutter. And that, darling daughter, would have made you crazy."

Oh mom, I thought. You know me too well.

Bounce Boost

There's something I like to call Survival of the Grateful-est. It's kind of like survival of the fittest, but better. It's good to be fit, but it's crucial to be grateful. It's particularly crucial to be grateful at those times when it seems there is absolutely nothing to be grateful for. Your house burns down, your spouse is diagnosed with cancer, you lose the job you've given your life to. Dear God, what could you possibly find in any of those situations to be thankful for?
A lot.

>Your family was out of the house at the time.

>Your spouse has a good oncologist.

>You're free to make a fresh start.

>I know from personal experience how hard it is to see the silver lining in such clouds, and I know how angry one can get at the mere suggestion of looking for a positive in a tsunami of negatives.

>*You want me to find something good in the fact that my spouse is in the Oncology ward again, Susan? Are you serious?*

>In the midst of the crisis we're certain there is nothing to be thankful for so we cry, we can't sleep, we curse God or the Universe for the shit that's befallen us.

We exhaust ourselves at the very moment we most need strength.

The way to that strength is gratitude. And the way to find something to be grateful for, is to look for it:

You awaken in the hospital next to your husband's bed after what feels like and probably is an entire 45-minutes of sleep, and the nurse hands you a fresh towel, toothpaste and a toothbrush and says, "Go, freshen up, I've got him."

Right there, that's your moment to be grateful – for the nurse, the toothpaste (thank God for the toothpaste!), the chance to take a quick shower and get your shit together. Don't miss that moment. Stop and see that moment, absorb it, be thankful for it, and it will fuel you.

That cabinet in my kitchen? My mom was absolutely right; I should have been grateful for it. It didn't fall off the wall, and its door didn't come unhinged. If it had, I might not have been far behind. My mom is a professional gratitude practitioner, and I mean that with the utmost respect. When the flowers she's had on her dining room table for two weeks finally have to go, she thanks them for bringing their beauty into her home before throwing them away.

Every morning when she wakes up, she says good morning to her house and, when she takes her first sip of coffee, she thanks God, not just for the coffee's warmth and deliciousness, but because she is alive to enjoy it.

Zig Ziglar once said, "The more you express gratitude for what you have, the more likely you will have even more to express gratitude for." This is especially true when everything in our lives has been turned upside down. Gratitude is the key to transcending tragedy. It is the key to finding strength in those moments, those marathon-long moments, when we need it most. And it is the only way to not just bounce back, but to bounce forward.

All Decisions Made by the Management Are Final
(Even If They're Not Popular)

As I mentioned earlier, the day we spread Stu's ashes went about as well as the day of his memorial service.

It rained buckets that day. I'm talking the kind of teeming, driving rain that whisks animals, neglected toys, and lawn furniture away, the kind of rain that soaks you to the skin, corkscrews a pin straight, overpriced blow-out, and makes so much mud your sensible black pumps get sucked straight off your feet in the five seconds it takes to get from the house to the car. Looking back now, I guess it was really the kind of rain you'd expect, but hope not to have, the day of a memorial service.

I know I hoped not to have it. But then, knowing what I know, I'm surprised it wasn't worse.

A month earlier, while he lay dying in his hospital bed, in our den, staring blankly at episode after episode of Pawn Stars which I was certain was hastening his demise and which I once, and only once, made the mistake of trying to change to a music channel only to have him suddenly brighten and nearly bean me with the remote,

Stu said, "Susan A., no service." His voice was really soft for someone still strong enough to close for Nolan Ryan, and for a second I thought what I always thought when he said this, *I'll pretend I didn't hear him.*

I looked at him. He was watching Rick go after Corey about some piece of crap the kid shouldn't have bought. A minute went by, then two. I thought he'd fallen asleep, so, very quietly I got up to start dinner. Obviously, I wasn't quiet enough. My butt wasn't two inches off the sofa when he suddenly said, "Susan A., did you hear me? No service."

"Yes, sweetheart," I said, going to him. "I heard you." And then I bent down, kissed him, and lied straight to his still so handsome face. "No service."

"I don't want to inconvenience everyone."

"I know," I replied. "But-"

He cut me off. "Death is very inconvenient, Susan."

Then how 'bout you don't die, I thought, looking at him, *and we go back to our lives.* You, loving the five-hundred-acre petting zoo we call home. Me, poking fun of it with every word I write. You, coaching football and letting Tug, our perpetually filthy golden retriever, get in our bed. Me, threatening to beat you and that hound with a helmet the next time I found cow manure all over my pillow.

Death is more than very inconvenient, I thought. Death sucks. Cancer sucks. And lying to a dying cancer patient to whom you've been married for almost twenty-two years and with whom you fundamentally disagree on the purpose of a service, well that really sucks.

"A service is for the living," said my mom.

"The kids need closure," said one of my girlfriends.

"Susan, he won't be here. For God's sake, do what you need to do to take care of yourself and your sons," said my therapist, Ellen.

My poor sons. Two kids so undone by the fact that no amount of taking out the garbage, making their beds, setting the table, getting good grades, or hosing down the dogs was going to save their dad, and who asked, begged really, on several occasions that we not be alone when the inevitable happened.

I promised them not to worry; we'd be surrounded by family and friends. And, when the boys were out of earshot, I promised Stu there'd be nothing but a simple obituary and that no one would ever utter the words, "Dammit! I'm going to miss the big game/party/annual sale at my favorite store because I have to go to McCorkindale's stupid service!"

Please, somebody tell me it's ok to be a two-faced, double-talking liar if you do it out of love.

In the end though, I know he got me.

We awakened the Saturday morning of his service to a veritable monsoon. Standing on the front porch, I watched a toad, a baseball mitt, and the pillow from our hammock whoosh away in what used to be a stream but was now a small tsunami. On our way to the funeral home, I lost a shoe in the mud and got so soaked trying to free it that I had to hit my hair with a blow dryer and a flat iron in the ladies' room. Yes, I did that. But only because Stu hated when I wore my hair curly even more than he hated the idea of a memorial service. I couldn't completely let him down.

And then, later that day, after two incredibly moving speeches from two of the dozens of young men my husband had coached and a brief but beautiful statement from my brother-in-law thanking everyone in attendance for taking such good care of us during his brother's illness, about sixty people joined us at our house for his repast.

It was quite the repast.

People eating and drinking and telling funny Stu stories. Kids racing in and out, soaking wet and covered in mud from playing manhunt in the still raging monsoon. The whole house ablaze with light and love and laughter – right up until the moment the windows on the front door blew in from the wind.

"Holy shit!" cried Cuy, appearing suddenly at my side clutching what was probably the last of our dry towels. "What happened?"

"The wind blew out the windows," I responded, watching four of Stu's friends duke it out with the door, finally securing it with almost an entire roll of duct tape.

"The wind, huh?" He shot me a look.

"That's my story and I'm sticking to it," I smiled. "Bring me the vacuum?"

He nodded and walked off toward the kitchen. It was when I heard him shout, "Guys! Guys! We can share this one, it's dry!" that I knew I'd be getting the vacuum myself. I also knew that, for better or worse, from this point forward I'd be making all the decisions myself.

Some of which apparently were not going to be too popular.

When the going gets tough, the tough email mom

TO: Mom

FR: Susan

SUBJECT: The real danger of sleep deprivation

Hi Mom,

It's three-fifteen in the morning and I'm awake and reading the "7 Little Known Dangers of Sleep Deprivation." It was one of the stories on MSN.com, so I clicked through. I guess I could be reading about a 132-pound toddler, reviewing the many and mind-numbing celebrity splits this month, or finding out the "5 Things You Didn't Know About Nick" (Jonas, in case you didn't know), but the sleep deprivation piece seemed more appropriate.

See? I can't be that sleep deprived. I still know what's appropriate.

In any case, the article says that:

The 7th little known danger of sleep deprivation is the impact it has on memory and concentration. And maybe it does. I can't remember.

The 6th little known danger is mental problems. Now that's a load of malarkey. We both know I had those way back when I slept through the night like a normal person.

The 5th little known danger is weight gain. Of course, it is. I'm awake because I'm sick with grief and wracked with anxiety. Let's punish me with some extra pounds!

The 4th little known danger is impaired decision-making skills. Hmm. I'm writing to you which is only going to make you worry more than you're already worrying so, yeah, they may have a point.

The 3rd and 2nd little known dangers are increased risk of work and auto accidents. Nope. Not me. Whether I get three hours of sleep or eight, you can count on me to sit down at a meeting, reach into my purse for a pen and pull out a tampon or misjudge the distance between the Durango and a dumpster. You saw the dent, right? I still haven't had it fixed.

As for the #1 little known danger of sleep deprivation? You're going love this, mom. It's illness. Colds, flu, even cancer.

Cancer.

I can't sleep because I can't stop thinking about Stu and how nothing we did could save him from cancer and this increases the possibility of my getting it, too?

They're wrong, you know.

The real #1 little known danger of sleep deprivation is my discovering who developed this damn list.

Love you,

Susan

Bounce Boost

One of my favorite things to do is to pay for the person behind me at the Starbucks drive thru. One of my other favorite things is when someone surprises me the same way. It makes me so happy, I start calling people.

"The driver behind me just bought my latte!" I say. "Oh my goodness, what a sweet thing to do!"

I'm not kidding; I respond like I just won the lottery and can't wait to spread the wealth. One time I got right back in line and ordered a slice of banana bread just so I could pay the "just won a million bucks" feeling forward immediately. Of course Robert's take on this is a bit different. He insists that the only people who do this are men when they see a beautiful woman in their rearview mirror. I hadn't thought of that and I'm pretty certain I disagree, but I appreciate the compliment.

There are some things, though, that I don't like paying forward.

The email I sent my mom? I knew while I was writing it that sharing my anger, anxiety and grief in a note written in the middle of the night was only going to make her worry more than she already was.

And still I did it.

She called me several hours later (at some human time, like 10 a.m.), to say she received the email and ask if I ever got any sleep, and I started to apologize.

"Sue," she said, "if you can't vent to me, who can you vent to? And besides, it was funny. I'm proud of you that you can laugh, it's a good sign. And while I don't like the idea of you tracking down whoever came up with that list, I'm happy to help."

You've got to love my mom.

Sure, there's stuff we shouldn't pay forward. But when we do, we need to cut ourselves some slack. We do it for other people. Why not do it for ourselves too?

Not the Usual Routine

One morning, while I was alternately straightening out Casey's closet, folding and re-folding the clothes in his dresser drawers, decluttering the top of his desk and dusting his bookshelves, the thought occurred to me that I was swirling through the house like the Tasmanian Devil on the Bugs Bunny cartoons I used to watch when I was a kid. *Pretty accurate*, I thought, closing the last drawer, and moving on to the check-for-dust-bunnies-under-the-bed portion of my non-stop program. I was down on my hands and knees, the bed skirt shoved over my head, maneuvering my dust rag in the semi darkness when I thought, *Actually, I'm worse than the Tasmanian Devil. I'm like the Tasmanian Devil on drugs.*

And then it hit me: when was the last time I'd taken *my* drugs?

Since the day my mom went home, shortly after Stu's service, I was on fast forward. I spent all day every day sweeping dog hair and dirt off the stairs and the kitchen floor, doing load after load of laundry, vacuuming, cleaning the bathrooms and the bedrooms, and doing dishes. So many dishes my hands cracked and bled while my dishwasher sat empty and staring at me like I'd lost my mind.

I sat back on my heels and wracked my brain.

When was the last time I'd taken my medication? The antidepressant with the lovely antianxiety component that, on one hand, keeps me from plummeting down the rabbit hole and on the other, stops me from becoming a perpetual motion machine convinced I can repaint the windowsills in the kitchen and brush my teeth at the same time.

In all the time Stu was sick, I'd never missed a dose. It was part of my routine: Up at four, make coffee, take meds, write until six, workout until seven, check on Stu, get the kids up, fed, and on the bus before eight, shower, dress, and get down to the kitchen to dole out whatever pain medication was working at the moment, race back upstairs to deliver it and ask if he wanted breakfast. He almost never wanted breakfast. He wanted sleep, so he'd go back to sleep, and I'd stand there for a while watching him and missing him in preparation for missing him.

The rest of my day was spent in a similar fashion. Delivering medications, encouraging him to eat, watching him sleep, and making appointments, maintaining the log I kept for his oncologist, calling the insurance company to confirm his approval for some upcoming procedure, filing medical bills, and requesting refills from the pharmacy.

Unless my husband was in the hospital, that was my day every day.

Now he was gone, and the schedule I'd clung to like a lifeline in cancer's churning sea of chaos and anxiety, dashed hopes, failed treatments, exhaustion and tests and trips to the emergency room in the middle of the night, and scared kids and missed school days and the indescribable fear that threatened to swallow my family, was no longer necessary.

My husband was dead. My manuscript was off to the publisher. And the routine that had given me structure, made me focus, and forced me to keep putting one foot in front of the other, evaporated like mist the morning he passed away. Now my day, every day, was unstructured, and I was unmoored. I kept moving to keep the panic at bay, to try and force time to pass more quickly (and do its healing thing already, dammit!), and because I couldn't stop myself.

That's it, I thought, watching a crack in the middle of my knuckle bleed onto the dust rag in my hand. *That's this, this frenzy.* I looked from Casey's now perfectly appointed closet and desk to his dresser with the perfectly straightened drawers that hadn't needed to be straightened. *Oh my God, Susan,* I thought. *All this frantic activity, the organizing and cleaning out, the dishes and the dusting and the laundry and the sweeping; how did you not see it?*

I had no idea, and I had to laugh because I'm so damned textbook. For me, grief plus no meds equals manic. That's it. That's been the bottom line my entire life. Suffer a heartbreak? Clean out my makeup drawer, overhaul my closet, try on all my clothes and shoes and boots and stuff a third of it in a bag for Goodwill. Vacuum my room, clean the windows and the mirrors, dust the dresser, the baseboards, the light fixture on the ceiling, even the lightbulbs in the lamps. Once when I was in high school, my mom poked her head in my bedroom door and asked if, when I was done, I'd do the living room and I said yes. (Yes! I was a teenager at the time; how did no one think my response warranted an emergency psych consult?) Perpetual motion is my default setting when something hurts so bad, I have two choices: scratch myself out of my skin or let loose on my surroundings. I know this about myself the same way I know that the sky is blue, the grass is green, and that it will take my son less than thirty seconds to return his closet to its original condition.

I know something else, too. I know I was lucky. The terrible high I was riding could have snowballed and taken on a life of its own, tricking me first into believing I had no time to eat, and soon after into not being hungry so why bother, all the while flooding me with so much cortisol I'd ultimately be left exhausted, physically sick, too thin to think straight, and curled up in a ball in a corner of the couch.

Thank God that didn't happen. I can't imagine my sons seeing me that way.

I stood up, collected the cleaning supplies scattered around Case's room, and brought them down to the kitchen. I never kept my prescriptions, vitamins, or antidepressant in the former McPharmacy for fear they'd get mixed up with Stu's stuff and make him sick or, maybe I should say, sicker, if that was even possible. My things were tucked in the cabinet closest to the refrigerator, in a back corner surrounded by my favorite mugs: a cheerful orange and white one I found at T.J. Maxx and had to have because orange makes me happy; a white one imprinted with the funniest self-portrait of Cuyler dressed in what I think he thought made him look like a Redcoat, but to me looks like a costume from the Sergeant Pepper's Lonely Hearts Club Band album cover; and a clear glass cup marked with three lines of text that say, "Shh," "Almost," and "Now you may speak," which is my favorite, despite the fact that no one's ever up to speak with me at four in the morning.

Every morning when I started my coffee, I'd open the cabinet, grab a cup, see my medication, and take it. But since the McPharmacy had been restored to its rightful role as a regular old kitchen cabinet and was now filled with Stu's favorite mugs – including the previously mentioned birdbath-size Bucknell University cup that can hold an awful lot of coffee – I'd been going to that cabinet and using that mug and, as a result, completely forgetting to take my antidepressant.

I took my pills. It would be about ten days before the Tasmanian Devil departed the premises, but it was sort of a relief to hand him his walking papers. I say sort of because soon the little serotonin reuptake inhibitors in my brain would regulate themselves, resetting my system from fast-forward to play. The panic would subside. I'd stop running. I'd start feeling.

It was not going to be pretty.

It would, however, be a step in the right direction.

All the frenzied motion kept a lid on my grief. It would be a relief to let it out and let myself miss Stu. And it would be wonderful to be able to sit in his library without a dust cloth clutched in my hands and look at his photos and his books, his Marines and New York Giants memorabilia, his Civil War and baseball collectibles. It would be wonderful to visit with his things and, in a way, him, for the first time in a long time.

So Much for Self-diagnosis

When was the last time you got two hours with your doctor? And no, Saturday at the school Science Fair with your respective kids in tow doesn't count. I mean in the office. You know, the room with the framed, dust covered diplomas on the walls, spindly philodendrons on the windowsill, family pictures crammed among dozens of foreboding medical journals on the disheveled bookshelves, and a desk buried beneath piles of manila folders so fat they cold crush a housecat.

Of course you don't know you're going to get two uninterrupted hours with the doctor. It just works out that way. At least it did for me on a long-ago day in 2002.

I went in for my appointment which began, of course, with me begging to pee before they forced me to step on the scale, moved quickly to a cry of "Is this thing accurate?" and ultimately found me sitting half naked on the examining table, freezing, and trying not to shred what amounted to an oversize tissue that the nurse insisted I slip into. With the opening in the back. Or maybe she said the front. I couldn't remember. I was cold. Not to mention fat. And in no condition to stop a Kleenex from achieving its lifelong goal of becoming confetti, streamers, and all manner of party decorations before the doctor came in.

When he finally did, after I'd cooled my heels and froze my butt for about twenty minutes, I figured I had ten minutes with him, fifteen at best, so I started running through my list of symptoms as soon as he said hello.

"This isn't like me, Dr. F.," I began. "I'm physically exhausted, but my thoughts keep bouncing around like a game of bumper pool in my brain."

He had his stethoscope on my upper back, and it was so cold I swear it was poking through a rip in the godforsaken gown. "Take a deep breath, Mrs. McCorkindale."

"I can barely get out of bed in the morning," I continued, craning my head around to try to look at him. "No energy whatsoever. It's as if I'm defeated before the day begins."

"And another."

"I'm gaining weight, too. Which I'm sure you saw. My dad had an overactive thyroid. When he was little, he was super skinny, so they took it out."

"And another." Great, he was listening to my kidneys and the gown was splitting right above my rear end.

"You should see the scar; looks like a choker. I'll bet mine's under active, isn't it? That's got to be why I'm getting fat. Should we take it out?"

"Last one. Big breath now." Thank God. One more second and my butt was going to make its debut.

"I don't really want a huge scar like my dad's, but I've got to feel better. I've got kids. I can't be falling asleep pouring their cereal." He put his stethoscope around his neck and patted the pocket of his lab coat. "And my body hurts. Really hurts. So bad my arms ache." I shut up for a second thinking he might actually examine my arms, but no. He just pulled out a pen, wrote something in my file, and picked up what looked like a penlight from a rack on the wall.

"Look straight at the light, please."

"No kidding, I have pain right down to my bones. It's so bad even the soles of my feet hurt.

"Follow it, eyes only, to the right."

"My grandmother had bone cancer. My dad's mom. Pretty screwed-up side of the family health-wise, now that I think about it."

"Now left."

"Anyway, she went to a chiropractor and they told her she had a bad back. A sprain or something." In one fell swoop, the penlight went back on the rack and he unwrapped a tongue depressor faster than my kids pull open a pop sickle.

"But she didn't have a bad back."

"Stick your tongue out for me, please."

"It wath bone canther!"

"Say 'Ah'"

"Ahhh."

He tossed the tongue depressor, wrote something in my file, and moved to the right side of the examining table.

"Right arm, please."

"Can you believe that quack? You don't think I have bone cancer, do you?" I'm not a fan of blood pressure cuffs, particularly when my arms hurt like hell. But I figured if he needed the info in order to rule out something lovely like the Plague, I could put up with the pain.

"Oh, oh, and I'm always sweating and then freezing, freezing and then sweating. In the space of, like, five minutes. The other day I was so cold, I had to borrow someone's sweater to put on top of my suit jacket. And then, not two minutes later, I could hardly breathe. It was like I was choking. My chest was tight. And my heart was racing so fast and hard, I thought everyone in the room could hear it.

"Blood pressure's good."

"And the sweat. Just pouring down the back of my neck." He held my wrist and we both watched the second hand go around the wall clock. "I ripped off the sweater and my jacket and, had it been all women, I'd have stripped to my bra. I'm telling you; it was that bad."

"Pulse is fine."

"I'll bet it's a flu of some kind. Or maybe a virus. And you can't do anything about either, right? Just have to rest, wait it out, drink fluids. Right?" I stared at my socks while he wrote in my file. "Yeah, it's got to be a flu bug. Wow. I can't believe I didn't think of it sooner. I'm so sorry I wasted your time."

I clutched what was left of the tissue to my body and waited for him to tell me to get dressed. I mean, I was done wasn't I? I'd listed my symptoms as fast as possible and even reached my own diagnosis. I was the poster patient for managed care. All I needed to do now was fork over my thirty bucks and be on my way.

Except that my doctor wasn't hustling me out of there. He was leaning against the counter, looking at me over his gold framed glasses, and nodding.

"Thyroid, huh?" he finally said. "Flu, bone cancer. Interesting calls. Where'd you get your M.D.?" He smiled. "Ok. We're going to draw some blood, then you and I are going to talk." He tucked his pen in the pocket of his lab coat and walked to the door. "Why don't you take a moment to read this while I get the nurse?" He pointed to a poster I'd noticed but paid no attention to, then ducked out.

He wanted to talk? There's no talking to the doctor. *These are the co-pay days!* Oh this was way worse than bone cancer. This was stage four Ebola at best.

I ditched the tissue and got dressed. It was only when I sat to pull on my boots that I remembered the poster. The one that said Warning Signs of Major Depression in huge letters across the top.

Was he kidding me? I had the flu, plain and simple. Or maybe a thyroid problem. *I'm tired, teary, and starting to look like a Tellatubby*, I thought. Definitely a thyroid problem. The blood test would prove it. I offered my right arm to the nurse and closed my eyes.

"He's in his office." She said, applying a band aid. "Go on in."

I hesitated. "I've been here awhile already. I'm sure he's got people waiting. Maybe he can just give me a prescription and I'll go.

Ok?" I'd been there close to forty minutes. The specialist I saw for my first pregnancy, a high-risk endeavor that had Stu and me freaking out and doing everything by the book to ensure Casey was healthy, never gave me more than fifteen minutes, tops. I was an overtired working mom with a lot on my mind. Everyone's thoughts race, right? I probably just needed a nap. Did we need to chat about it?

"You're in luck. We've had a couple of cancellations. He has plenty of time."

****

"So, what's been going on?" He swung into the office and closed the door, revealing yet another copy of the depressing depression poster that I only semi scanned in the examining room. I had the feeling he was going to give me one as a parting gift.

"Just what I told you. Sometimes I can't sleep. Other times, all I want is sleep. One minute I'm really happy, and the next I'm a raging crazy woman. Or I'm crying. I feel like I have permanent PMS." He gave me a small smile and the patented doctor look that says *go on* without uttering a single syllable and tapped his pen on my file folder. "I can't think straight, you know? I'm all over the place. Mostly I'm tired and fat. I'm thinking it's my thyroid. What do you think?"

"You still working for yourself?" Now he was flipping through the file, occasionally stopping to scan one of his old notes. "I think you once told me you work from home, right?" He closed the folder and look at me, expectantly.

"I did. But not anymore. Recession killed my business." What did this have to do with my thyroid?

He shook his head and looked me straight in the eye. "That had to be tough. You worked for yourself a long time, at least as long as you've been my patient."

The lump that rose in my throat and the tears that stung my eyes took me totally by surprise. This wasn't a topic I wanted to talk about. Ten years as a self-employed, successful advertising copywriter. Awesome clients. The freedom to do the work I loved anywhere I wanted to: home, the shore, even the maternity ward at

Hackensack Hospital. All of it gone with the recession that began the banner year of 2001.

"It's ok," I lied. "I got a job pretty quick. I was lucky." I really was lucky. My friend Trish had been interviewing for the top marketing spot at a national men's magazine on the morning of September 11th. She landed it, met up with her husband who'd made it safely out of the Wall Street area, and raced home to hug her kids and call her parents. And me. She offered me a senior position on her staff, and I took it. No interviews. No haggling. None of the usual, nerve wracking preliminaries. Just a gift, an absolutely incredible gift, from one girlfriend to another.

And so, sometime in mid-September, amid the missing person posters and the shrines to fallen firefighters and the police barricades and the daily funeral processions in front of St. Patrick's Cathedral, I went back to work in New York.

"So not too much time to mourn, huh?"

I rooted around my bag for a tissue, silently berating myself for not keeping a few shreds of that stupid gown. "Mourning is a luxury I can't afford right now. I have a mortgage to pay, kids to feed and clothe and," my voice cracked, "you know, buy birthday presents for." *Dammit.* How could I have car keys, gum, a nail file, even one of Cuyler's Matchbox cars, but no tissues? And the better question: how could I move this painful interrogation along to the prescription portion of the program?

He offered me a tissue and I took one. Then he asked how Stu was doing, and I took three more.

"Ok, I guess. Home with the boys. Coaching junior football. Underemployed." I paused to confer with my Kleenex. "I worry about him." I really didn't want to go into this stuff. Stu was working at home, when there was any work, and pretending to be happy. I was in the city, often overwhelmed with work, and pretending to be happy. We didn't discuss it, though. We just got up every day and did what we had to do. I joked to my girlfriends that we didn't have battle fatigue. We had fake-it fatigue.

"So what do you think," I probed, desperate to move of the conversation in the direction of medication. "Thyroid, right?"

"We'll run the blood work to be sure, but no. I'm ninety-nine-point-nine percent certain it's not your thyroid." He rocked back in his chair, pressed his palms together and put them to his lips, like he was praying. "Let me ask you this," he said. "Obviously, you have a lot on your plate, and it sounds to me like you haven't been feeling well for a while. To my way of thinking you really should have come in sooner. But you didn't. So what prompted you to finally make this appointment?"

I looked around. He had a diploma from Cornell, a bunch of certificates from the AMA, and some dusty family photos. And of course there was that pesky depression poster which I decided, suddenly, to study, in a desperate attempt to dodge his question.

Not even two bullets down, I regretted my decision.

Warning Signs of Major Depression

- decreased energy, fatigue, feeling "slowed down"

Check.

- thoughts of death or suicide, or suicide attempts

Shit. Check.

- difficulty concentrating, remembering, or making decisions
- persistent sad, anxious, or "empty" mood
- loss of interest or pleasure in activities, including sex

Shit. Shit. Shit.

- restlessness, irritability, or excessive crying
- feelings of guilt, worthlessness, helplessness, hopelessness, pessimism
- sleeping too much or too little, early-morning awakening

Check. Check. Check.

- appetite and/or weight loss or overeating and weight gain

Oink.

- persistent physical symptoms that do not respond to treatment, such as headaches, digestive disorders, and chronic pain

Ah ha! See? No way. Not me!

"How dare you accuse me of having headaches, digestive disorders, and chronic pain!" I said, pointing to the last line and pretending to be angry. I tried to laugh but it wasn't funny. I felt caught, spied on, stunned. The only thing the poster was missing was my picture.

I was starting to feel like I was at a Depressives Anonymous meeting. *Hi, my name is Susan and I suffer from depression.*

"So it's not my thyroid."

He shook his head.

"And it's not the flu."

He shook his head again.

"And you'd still like me to tell you why I made this appointment, wouldn't you?"

A nod on his part, a big breath on mine, and I told him about the past few weeks. How every day when I'm in the city I think about how easy it would be to step out into the bus lane. How just a few days ago, I stood on the very edge of the curb, leaned out into the street, and let a bus blow past me so close I could have reached out and touched it.

"I don't think I'd do it," I said. "I'd miss my boys too much. But I can't stop thinking about it."

And then to my great surprise and even greater relief, he told me he knew what I was talking about. That there was a time in his life when he felt like I've been feeling. And then he told me he could help me.

Hallelujah! We'd reached the prescription portion of the program!

And then he did indeed write something on his prescription pad. It was a woman's name, followed by her phone number.

Uh, hello? Something in pill form please?

"When it comes to therapists, she's the gold standard." He paused. "Do the work, and you'll get well."

What work? I was well. I just spent two hours talking to him. Hell, I was healed! I didn't want a therapist. I wanted a pill and to put this all behind me.

"But I don't need a shrink, Dr. F., I–"

"Oh, she's not a shrink. She's a therapist. But she'll recommend a shrink, I'm sure. The best course is typically talk therapy in combination with medication."

Oh dear God. How was I going to explain this to my parents? We're not therapy people; we're Catholics. The closest we come is Confession. We don't any feel better, but the price is right. And how should I tell Stu? *Hey honey, you'll never believe it, but I've found Freud. Yeah, yeah, you didn't know he was missing. Good one.*

This was going to get messy. Messier than colliding with the M10 bus? Maybe not. But it was going to come close.

"I'm going to buzz her now and let her know she can expect to hear from you this afternoon." He stood and reached out to shake my hand; his face filled with genuine concern. "So please, call. And Mrs. McCorkindale?"

"Yes?"

"Stay on the sidewalk."

Bounce Boost

Long before Stu's diagnosis I'd begun work on my second book. It didn't have to be finished for about a year, and my plan was to take my time filling it with more stories of my fish-out-of-water life on the farm. Things like my affinity for celebrating the holidays by attaching battery-operated Christmas lights to the ear-tags of our heifers, and the day I unintentionally killed a chicken by hitting it in the head with the root ball of a dead pansy. In my defense, the chicken and her pals dug up the pansies five minutes after I planted them so, yes, I was a little annoyed, but I didn't mean to kill her and, as it turned out, I didn't. The poor girl was ill – which we didn't know – and my beaning her with the root ball was simply the straw that broke the bantam's back. So to speak.

While Stu was out on the farm and the boys were in school, I wrote. Of course, I did mom stuff too: laundry and housework, figured out what to make for dinner, and hosed down the dogs more times than I care to recall but, for the most part, I sat at my desk doing my thing. It was such a gift to be able to spend all day doing what I love.

That luxury stopped and my aforementioned "up at four, make coffee, take meds, write until six, etc." routine started the instant my husband's cancer diagnosis was confirmed. It was tough at first to get into that groove, because it meant acknowledging that what was happening was real. But I'd set my alarm for four and rocket out of bed when it went off. If I hesitated for just a second, I'd start to panic, and I had no time for that. I had a husband to take care of, kids who needed to see me strong and in charge despite the circumstances. And I had a book to finish.

Thank God for that book. For two hours every morning, writing that book gave me something else to focus on. And, as it got closer to the publication date and I made my final edits to chapters I'd written months and months before Stu got sick, it was an escape, like a mini vacation every day to go back in time and visit our lives, my life, before cancer. I'd awaken on empty and leave my desk two hours later completely refueled and ready to take on whatever the day decided to bring.

When you're going through hell the only thing you can do is keep going, and to keep going, you've got to take care of yourself.

Even if it's just for fifteen minutes every day, paint, write, go for a walk, call a friend, read a book.

You can't pour from an empty vessel. Do something that fuels you.

Death's Not Up for Discussion

Rumor has it that other people talk about the deaths of their spouses. And I mean specifics about the day, the night, the morning the person died. The sticky, sweet smell in the room, the way the light from the baby monitor glowed red and relentless on a table overflowing with pills and drops and nurse's notes, the ping of the pain pump going off for the three hundredth time, despite the fact that they've laid there, on the floor, next to the hospital bed all night, clutching a box of D batteries and putting them in ahead of schedule so there'd be no break in the Fentanyl drip doing its best but, ultimately, not enough, to keep their spouse comfortable.

What it was like. You know, the details.

You never talk about the night Stu died.

My grief counselor, Laurie, and I were sitting in my cold kitchen sipping hot, super sweet tea a few days after the one-year anniversary of Stu's death when she just kind of casually slipped that in there and then looked at me like, So?

"Are you kidding with me?" I replied. I mean, why in God's name would I talk about that? I try not to even think about it. "People talk about that?"

"Most of the time it's all they talk about."

I got up to get more honey. I find the grief counseling goes down better with a spoonful of sugar or, better yet, a bottle of Chardonnay. But only if the session's after five.

"Really?" I replied. "People spend all their time talking about the night my husband died?"

"Ah, humor." She smiled. "How handy."

Truth is, it was morning, and I don't talk about it. I just wait until it pops into my consciousness, unbidden, and sucker punches me in the stomach while I'm unloading the dishwasher, doing laundry, or driving, getting my roots done, buying groceries, or trying to put two words together. The worst, though, is when I'm doing something like watching Cuy make a big play during a flag football game and, swept up in the moment, turn and shout "Did you see that, sweetheart?" to one of my girlfriends or, more mortifyingly, one of their husbands.

Yeah, that really hurts.

Of course if I did talk about Stu's death, I'd have to admit that on the last afternoon of his life, I ran out of Atropine. Atropine keeps the fluid in a dying person's lungs from building and making what's called a death rattle. Rattle, my ass. A space shuttle launch makes less noise. I'd hit the pain pump every thirty minutes or so, pray it would work, and then, just as the tension began to leave his face, that damn sound would burst from his throat and he'd be awake, agitated, and in pain. Again.

And so, because after nearly two years as a cancer caregiver I had it in my head that I now had a medical degree, I concluded that additional drops of Atropine would do the trick. And they did, until I ran out and panicked.

I jumped in the car with Casey, leaving my mom and Cuyler in charge, and raced to the pharmacy. The Fentanyl was working.

The last dose of Atropine was working. I thought I had at least twenty minutes.

I thought wrong.

Not halfway there my cell phone rang. The caller ID flashed "Home," and instantly I knew we were about to begin the longest night in any of our lives.

"Where are you?" Cuyler cried. "Come home! It's happening!"

I remember begging God not to let me and Casey get killed as I did a million point turn on the narrow road with a ditch on one side and a ravine on the other, and racing back to find Cuy sitting on the porch, sobbing. I remember finding my mom trying to calm Stu who was awake and disoriented, and trying desperately to get at the pain pump. I remember the sound of footsteps on the stairs as both boys made a mad dash for the safety of their rooms.

And I remember the frightened, anguished looks on their faces when I screamed that they had to get the hell down here and help.

My mom tells me that, despite my memory of being completely panic-stricken, I was calm as I did everything the hospice aide taught me to do. I lowered the hospital bed flat, positioned her and Cuy on one side, and me and Casey on the other. Then the four of us grabbed the sheet under Stu and shoved him up the bed, until his head was just about hanging over the top. Then I raised the bed, so he was sitting bolt upright, and the rattling sound stopped.

I remember kissing both boys, and watching them run from the room, and calling hospice and having a nurse arrive about forty-minutes later with more Atropine. I remember my girlfriend's husband delivering the prescription I couldn't pick up sometime around seven.

And then I remember sitting on the floor of the den right next to the hospital bed, with the pain pump and the batteries and the Atropine and asking God what my poor husband could possibly have done to deserve this.

My favorite hospice nurse, Martha, arrived around midnight, and I slipped into bed next to Stu. I told him it was ok to let go, that I loved him, and would take care of the kids. I promised him they'd go to school and get good grades and that I'd do everything in my power to make them grow to be fine men, and never become Redskins fans. I know he heard me because he hugged me. And then Martha sent me to bed.

He died at five forty-one the next morning. He was sixty-one, whip smart, funny as hell, and the best-looking man I've ever laid eyes on. As for me, I still haven't gotten an answer from God, and I still don't know why anybody talks about this stuff.

Bounce Boost

There are no words to describe the pain of watching someone you love die, but there are plenty of words to describe the joy of living. Over the course of Stu's illness, we talked about life a lot. Specifically our life, together. We talked about our long-ago days as a couple and then as newlyweds. We talked about having Casey and thinking we'd created the perfect child because he never cried. And we talked about having Cuyler, who cried for the first three years of his life, and laughed recalling how thankful we were he was born second because if he'd come first? There'd be no Casey.

As time got shorter, we talked about what life would look like for me and the boys when he was gone, and we talked a lot about the two things he wanted the three of us never to forget – that he loved us, and he wanted us to live – right now, this minute, no waiting. Cancer was not to take all of us. This he made me promise him.

After Stu died, I was asked to address a group of people facing a similar situation. The event coordinator hoped I could give them some advice. Advice? From me? I'm not an expert at cancer care giving and I'm certainly not a grief counselor. What could I possibly say to them?

I said I'd do my best.

The night before the presentation, as I reread the drivel I'd written, I recalled the promise I made Stu. In that moment I realized that the only way to keep my word was to keep moving forward and approach life with open arms. And to live in that manner, to me, meant doing five things.

The advice I gave those lovely people became the basis of a talk I give called Five Do's and a Do-over. The Five Do's are my ways of living as if my life were ending tomorrow, and the Do-over is an example of something I wish I'd done differently. I share the Do's and the Do-over here because I believe it shouldn't take cancer or any of life's tragedies to wake us up to living right now, this minute, no waiting.

The Five Do's

#1. Do Love. Never miss the chance to tell someone you love them. Your mom, your kids, your spouse, the hair stylist who fixed the dye job you thought you could do yourself, the friend who de-skunked your dog so you wouldn't come home to it after a long day at the hospital. Life is short. If you love someone, tell them.

#2. Do Listen. The little voice telling you to buy the shoes and the bag, get the jet-black manicure, and learn to ride a horse? That's the one to listen to. You can always take the shoes and the bag back, the polish will last ten days, tops, and as long as the little voice isn't suggesting your ride bareback (and if it is, I suggest you stop putting Bailey's in your breakfast coffee), go for it.

#3. Do Leap. Maybe you've always wanted to see the Amalfi coast or try stand-up comedy.

Maybe you're itching to ditch your corporate gig to run a tiki bar or write the great American novel. It doesn't matter what you want to do, just that you do it. Don't wait for the time to be right, for someone else to give you permission or for all the pieces to be in place. The stars will never be a hundred percent aligned so leap, as the saying goes, and build your wings on the way down.

#4. Do Let Go. Anger, guilt, resentment, perfectionism, and shame are all crippling, soul-sucking emotions. Forgive others. Forgive yourself. And for Pete's sake, stop trying to be perfect. Flaws are the new black. Pass it on.

#5. Do Laugh. If you can't fix it, kill it, cure it or eradicate it from the face of the earth, you can laugh at it. And you should. People who laugh a lot tend to live longer. Laughter helps and heals. It makes the whole "life's a bitch" thing more bearable. Trust me on this.

And 1 Do-Over...

Not laughing, loving, listening, leaping, and letting go sooner. It took Stu's illness and subsequent death to make me realize how little time we really have, and how crucial it is to be present and grateful for each moment. I don't regret not getting to this point sooner (particularly since regret is one of those soul-sucking, crippling emotions I urge all of us to kiss off). I'm just happy to be here now.

Part Two

WHAT TO EXPECT WHEN YOU NEVER EXPECTED TO BE A WIDOW

"There are good days and there are bad days, and this is one of them."

Lawrence Welk

When Good Moms Go Dad

My first Mother's Day as a single mom or, more accurately, a widow with two kids, was, in no uncertain terms, weird. The boys' cards were sweet, but I missed the suggestive ones Stu used to give me. I confess, I always complained that they weren't romantic enough, but hell, they were hot. Wait, let me rephrase that. They made me feel hot. Young. Desirable. On my first Mother's Day as a single mom/widow, I certainly didn't feel hot, unless the mega flash I got walking around, looking at the crap in Kohl's while Case and Cuy saw a movie counts. And, please God, tell me it doesn't.

Instead I felt old. Tired. Angry at the stupid, fluffy girl stuff I was surrounded by. And surprised. I mean I *like* stupid, fluffy girl stuff. On previous Mother's Days I always wore something pretty and feminine to go to lunch with my men. This year though, I didn't have the appetite or the energy. I pulled on shorts and a tee shirt, paid for the boys' movie tickets and popcorn, and killed time first in the store and then in the car where I found myself daydreaming about going home and having the kids help wash the cars.

Weird right? Maybe Father's Day is more my holiday.

It wouldn't surprise me.

In the past month I've learned several manly things. For starters, I now know how to jump start and charge a car battery, check and replace the oil, coolant, and a couple of other liquids that, yeah, ok, I've forgotten the names of, but I can replace them. Really, I can. I've also discovered why reading the car manual is more important (but a lot less inspiring) than reading the new issue of *Real Simple*, and how having an extra pair of reading glasses in the glove compartment makes playing auto mechanic much easier.

In addition to engine maintenance, I've learned that rain is God's way of saying, "Get out there and wipe down the Mustang, missy; your husband's up here all apoplectic at the pollen covering his favorite convertible!" and that wiping down the car can very quickly become cleaning the car, which even more quickly can become waxing the car which quicker than quick gets one wondering, "What in hell is happening to my testosterone level?"

And that's not something I've wondered just once.

As it turns out, the black dots I discovered on my chest are not, thank Heaven, hair sprouting in response to my new hobbies, but rather two ticks I picked up in the throes of detail duty. Scary, I know. I mean, a woman with chest hair? What happens if it doesn't match my mustache?

In all seriousness, I'm rather proud of my new talents and I think if Stu were here he'd be proud of me too. Try as he did to teach me certain things while he was alive, it took his death to force me to figure out that…

1. The weirdly shaped watering cans lined up in our backyard have nothing to do with gardening and everything to do with grilling. Yes, after one particularly misguided and inventive laced attempt to pour the contents of what turned out to be a propane tank on the plants, I discovered that it was not in fact filled with Miracle Gro or any other kind of fertilizer for that matter, and that the only thing I'd get from my continuing efforts to puncture it would be the chance to win a Darwin Award.

2. If I want to barbecue anything for dinner, I need to keep the weirdly shaped watering cans, a.k.a. propane tanks, filled with propane. This requires bringing them to the gas station (who knew?) where the nice man takes my empty tank and gives me one of his full ones. This is very lovely of him, and I thank him profusely, but I don't want his tank. I want mine. My husband touched that tank! Who knows where his has been?

3. There's no need to feel proprietary about a propane tank. "Ma'am, I'm sorry about your husband but I swear, they're all the same."

Maybe Father's Day isn't my holiday, but I might as well give it a try. I've mastered a whole lot of Dad stuff lately so if you need to replace the gross, funky plunger piece in the toilet, snake a drain, caulk a leak, or cajole the router back to life before your kids kill themselves from lack of Internet access, never fear, Susan is here. I probably won't feel like getting dressed up or going to lunch that day either and I definitely won't want a beer like my Bud guy always did, but maybe I'll barbecue. The kids love steak. And they can have one right after they finish washing the cars.

I have a confession to make. . .

The Mother's Day card Cuy made me broke my heart. On the cover, he'd drawn a picture of me with pink crayon in his signature Redcoat-meets-Sgt.-Pepper's-Lonely-Hearts-Club-Band-style, so I rather resembled Ringo, and on the inside he'd written this poem. He gave me permission to share it here which is good because I can't help myself.

You're the bomb, Mom

Dear Mom,

For all your hard work and labor

I'd like to thank you for being my savior

I know it's been tough for you, Casey, and me

Ever since Dad died

Thank you for providing for your family

That was really manly

You are a funny writer

But an even better grief fighter

I know Casey is a real headache

And I'm not always a piece of cake

But you are the bomb

Thank you and Happy Mother's Day, Mom

Love,

Cuyler

Wine. It's What's for Breakfast

Cuyler and I are standing in the wine aisle in the Food Lion in Myrtle Beach, South Carolina. It's eight o'clock Sunday morning, and he's in a bathing suit, flip flops, a tee shirt that reads, "New Jersey: Only the Strong Survive," and a New York Giants cap. Except for two bags of Entenmenn's Pop 'ems powdered donuts and a pair of plastic swim goggles, there's nothing in our cart.

To our right is a young couple with a spikey haired toddler hollering "No stop! No stop!" and banging his head on the wheel of one of those big, plastic, red and yellow racecar carts moms and dads have hated since Fisher Price first rolled them off the assembly line and over some poor, sleep-deprived parents' foot. To our left is an older woman who's alternately reading the labels aloud and cursing because she can't find what she's looking for. "Dammit. Was it

Monkey Bay? Frog's Leap? Little Penguin? For shit's sake. It was *some* animal I wouldn't adopt, never mind drink."

Of course, I can't find what I'm looking for either and it doesn't help that Mr. Can We Please Get the Swim Goggles and Go? keeps moaning, "Come on, mom!"

I scan the shelves as fast as anybody who's driven ten hours and slept four can, grab two bottles of chardonnay, and plop them into the cart next to the Pop 'ems.

"The breakfast of champions," Cuy says smiling.

I laugh and invective lady shoots me a disapproving look, sniffs loudly, and storms off toward the produce department clutching a jug of Ernest and Julio Gallo.

"I don't think the Chablis gal has had her Wheaties yet," I stage whisper to Cuy and the mom with the kid in the big red car. I figure I'll get a giggle from her, but no. She looks at me like "Some people!" tugs on her husband's tank top, and then actually says, "Some people!" as she starts pushing their cart away.

Excuse me?

"I'm just being silly," I offer, feeling awful.

"Yeah," Cuy interjects sweetly. "She's just being silly." The humorless young mom and her equally funny bone-challenged better half look relieved. Right up until the moment my handsome son leans in toward theirs, winks, and whispers, "My mom's a huge kidder. There's no way she'd let me and my brother drink anything but beer before lunch."

We're awful, I know. But we're harmless.

As a way of explanation, I can only say, I'm a cutup. I come from a long line of cutups. My dad and my brothers David, Nick, and Dan are some of the fastest wits in the world. And then I married a cut-up. Stu was the master of the off the cuff comment and quick comeback; he just thoroughly enjoyed joking around. For almost twenty-two years of marriage, all I tried to do was keep up. And from the moment he died, all I've tried to do is keep it up.

Maybe it's a weird way to deal with grief, but it's our way. And I don't think we're that far off the mark. One of my all-time favorite quotes is, "If you can't make it better, you can laugh at it."

And I say, if you can laugh at it, you can live through it.

"You were a little over the top back there, Mom," Cuy teases at the register. The cashier's scanned his swim goggles and he's struggling to free them from the tamper-proof packaging that infuriates parents even more than having their feet run over by those damn Fisher Price shopping carts.

"Me?" I reply, pretending to take offense. "You're the one who made the whole 'beer with breakfast' comment to a toddler."

"There's a toddler drinking beer?" the cashier asks, popping onto her tiptoes and craning her head from side to side.

"No, there isn't," Cuy replies. "But there's going to be an 11-year-old guzzling one soon if I can't get these stupid things out."

"You a Bud guy, Cuy?" I laugh as the swim goggles explode from their nuclear attack proof plastic and cardboard wrapping, fly forward, land at the feet of invective lady who's checking out one lane over from us, and Cuy blurts out "Shit!"

In a flash he's retrieved them, put them on, and is standing next to me. Neither of us can stop laughing.

"Did she buy Wheaties?" I whisper.

"It was a rescue mission, not recon," Cuy laughs, moving the goggles to the top of his head for full surfer dude effect.

"Do you guys always have this good a time at the grocery store?" the cashier asks. I look at Cuy and his face says it all.

"Not always," he replies, "but we're getting better. Right, Mom?"

Everyday sweetheart. Everyday.

Little Gold Anchors. Away.

I can't remember the exact date I took my wedding rings off, which bothers me because I remember in minute detail the exact date (time, place, what I was wearing – white comes to mind) when I put them on, but I know it was sometime late in our first summer as a threesome.

Best I can recall, it was late summer, and my second book was about to come out. Our Durango and Mustang were taking turns breaking down and costing me thousands of dollars to repair, Borders had just folded which foreshadowed lousy sales and much less income to fix the aforementioned vehicles, and both Casey and Cuyler, still reeling from Stu's death, were undone at the prospect of losing me to a book tour. Add to this the fact that I spent most of every day muttering *I think I can, I think I can* under my breath like the little engine that could, and you can see why now, when I look back, it might not have been the best time to cut my little gold anchors. But I did.

It was morning and I was in our bedroom getting dressed and, like most women I know, reaching for the same jewelry I wear every single day. I say most women because Laurie, my grief counselor, is one of the few exceptions to that rule. She's always got on something different, and spectacular, and frequently handmade (by her, for God's sake) to match her outfit. I look at her all I can think is "How do you have the energy, woman?" She kills me.

But of course death, and my subsequent lack of energy (among other things), has everything to do with why I see a grief counselor in the first place.

But I digress.

I put in my big hoops, slipped on my collection of chunky bracelets that jangle and clang and make all manner of noise because no, my personality alone just isn't loud enough, and reached for my wedding rings. And then, as I've done every day for most of my adult life, I forced them up over my lumpy knuckle and slammed my jewelry drawer shut.

To be clear, it's only half a drawer. The other half is underwear, and it's an excellent setup until somebody just about gets her bellybutton pierced by an earring post. And yes, that happened. I was lunching with a friend when I suddenly got a sharp, stabbing pain in my stomach. As I have the worst stomach in recorded history, I chalked it up to more of the same. But later in the ladies' room I discovered the real culprit. Lodged in the lace of my underwear was a pointy little stud earring. And no, I haven't felt the same about saltwater pearls since.

But again, I digress.

At the exact moment I slammed the drawer, the boys started screaming at each other downstairs in the kitchen.

"No, it's your turn to take out the garbage!"

"I did it yesterday. It's your turn!"

They are so selfish! I thought, racing to the stairs, and taking them two at a time to the bottom.

"Guys," I hissed. "Keep it down! You're going to wake—" I stepped into the kitchen and stopped.

"Wake who, mom?" Casey demanded, looking both fed up with his brother and frightened for my mental health.

"I didn't say 'wake,'" I lied. "I said 'make.' You're going to make me angry. Now knock it off, both of you."

"She totally said 'wake,'" I heard Cuyler whisper as I went back upstairs.

Sure did, dude, I thought as I tugged off my rings and stuck them in a box. There was no one else in the house to wake up; no one else in the house to tell the boys to pipe down or talk with about the cars or the bills or even Borders. It was all me, and it hurt too much to continue pretending otherwise. I took a deep breath – and one last look at my little gold anchors – and tucked the box deep in the back of my jewelry drawer. Then I went down to deal with Big Ears and his brother.

At least I think that's what happened. Like I said, I really can't recall.

At Least I Know I'm Not Crazy

Allow me to clarify that statement. At least I know I'm not crazi*er*.

For the last month or so, I have been absolutely exhausted. I mean bone tired, barely able to lift my head up off my pillow. I sleep 'til six, or six-thirty, or even, on several occasions, seven. I know, you're laughing at me now. But really, if I sleep until five, I'm late. If I sleep until seven, please, check for a pulse.

And when I finally do wake up, with all this extra rest under my belt, am I refreshed? Energized? Bright eyed, bushy tailed, and ready to work, workout, and work some more? On the contrary. I feel like a sloth. On Seroquel. With a Sominex kicker.

I go to my desk and can hardly put two words together.

I drag myself to my Jazzercise class with the promise that, if I arrive early, I can catnap in the car before I go in.

I catnap.

I go in.

And I stand there, smiling and making small talk through waves of exhaustion-induced nausea and praying *Please, please, please God, don't let me collapse or worse, throw up, on the bouncy black floor.*

I'm telling you; it's been bizarre. In addition to my newfound ability to fall asleep anywhere, any time (including in the Orthodontist's office and in the car *on the way to* the Orthodontist's office which was really scary because I was the one driving), by lunchtime every day I've had a headache. After that, by two or three, my tongue's swollen and dotted with those awful little white bumps that hurt so bad you want to bite them off and spit them out. And then, because it's not enough that my head hurts, I'm desperate for sleep, and I'm practically eating Orajel, my day ends with a screaming sore throat. I've taken Tylenol. Gargled with warm salt water. And consumed shocking amounts of Chardonnay. Hey, it's alcohol, alcohol kills germs. And my thinking is off here… how?

Nothing helped.

In short order, I added waking up crying to my list of ills.

Now if I may digress for just a moment, I hate it when I wake up crying. Not because my pillowcase is streaked with mascara which always makes me feel like I failed girl school because I'm certain all of my friends manage to remove theirs every night before bed, or even because it makes it that much tougher to get my face up to snuff before I step out of the house. (Seriously, if I wake up crying, it takes cold cream, Q-tips, and the pointy end of my metal nail file in order to reclaim my crow's feet and the six-lane freeway running across my forehead. And I'm not even going to go into what it takes to bring my eyelids back from looking like boobs, though it is nice to finally have a pair.) No. I hate it when I wake up crying because it means I've been having this terrifying, recurring nightmare in which Stu is alive and sick and somehow I've forgotten to take care of him. The dream is always the same. I'm at a restaurant with friends and I'm looking at the menu. Suddenly, my cell phone rings. I pull it out of my purse and practically faint: Stu's name is on the caller ID. *Oh my God,* I think. *What have I done?* I race from the restaurant sick with panic, crying, and praying I'll get home to him in time. And then I wake up, still crying, and thanking God it was just a dream.

In any case, as far as I was concerned this crowning symptom screamed, "Susan, it's time for a psych consult."

"Your meds are fine," Ellen responded calmly when I called her and not so calmly begged for an increased dose of the antidepressant I take daily.

"But I feel awful," I moaned.

"Susan," she said soothingly, "you don't treat a sore throat with Celexa."

"Wellbutrin, then?" I asked, cutting her off. "Or maybe something new, like Paxil? Or Zoloft. I've never taken either one of those. What do you think?"

"I think you should call your doctor."

"But you *are* my doctor," I cried. "And I'm not sick. I'm depressed. I'm talkin' right down the rabbit hole. Do something!"

"Susan," she said, a little more firmly, "it's not your meds. Call your regular doctor and get some blood work done."

And then she hung up. Just like that. I hate tough love. I want to be coddled and told everything will be alright. In fact, I want it in writing.

On a prescription pad.

With at least two refills.

In the end, I did get a prescription. And believe it or not, it starts with a Z. As in Z-pack. I have strep throat and full-blown mono. Mono! Could it be some kind of cosmic payback for removing my wedding rings or yelling at big ears and his brother? I really don't know. But at least I do know why I've been feeling so awful. And it's not because I'm going crazy.

Allow me to clarify that statement…

Hell if I Know

According to the experts and by that, I mean *the* expert, renowned psychiatrist and author Elisabeth Kübler-Ross, there are five stages of grief: denial, anger, bargaining, depression, and acceptance.

In our case, Casey, Cuyler and I did most of our denying and bargaining over the course of Stu's almost two year battle with pancreatic cancer, but since his death, on any given day, at any given moment of the day, we've got anger, depression, and acceptance taking turns having their way with us.

We also have, and I respectfully suggest this as a sixth stage, hell.

Cuyler is obsessed with hell. Not because he thinks Stu is there, but because he's certain he's in Heaven and would really like to be sure he's spending eternity with people who earned their wings and didn't skate in on an apology after, say, an ethnic cleansing spree.

"Do you think Hitler is in Hell?" he asks me over dinner. "He has to be, right? But what if he stood before Saint Peter and told him he was sorry? And what if Saint Peter went and got God, and God looked deep into Hitler's soul and saw that he really, truly was sorry. And what if we all don't know it, but *God accepted Hitler's apology?* And Hitler? He's up there, right now, with nice people like Dad!"

I try to assure him that Hitler is enjoying an especially toasty spot in Hell, but he's not having any of it.

"Grandma says we're supposed to believe in a merciful God. Well if He really is merciful, maybe all the bad people just apologize and everyone gets in. And if everyone gets in, then Hell's a bunch of b.s." He pauses to pop a piece of steak in his mouth, then spits it back out spluttering, *Eew, fat!* "I half don't believe in Hell*th*," he says, running his tongue along the bottom of his top teeth in an attempt to scrape off the taste, "and I half do."

I begin to suggest that there are probably degrees to God's mercy and that somebody like Osama Bin Laden isn't just going to stroll up to the Pearly Gates, apologize, and get a pass, but this particular reference sends him right over the top.

"And that's the other thing about Hell," he says, slamming his knife onto his plate. "We really don't know who's calling the shots in Heaven, so for all we know we're all going to Hell. Think about it. If the Catholics control Heaven, do all the Jews go to Hell? And what if the Jews are in charge? Do the Catholics go? And can you imagine if, God forbid, the Taliban are in charge? We're all screwed."

"Burqas for everybody!" I tease.

Round and round he goes, trying to figure out who's controlling the hereafter and weighing the benefits of converting to that particular faith while there's still time. It's funny, in a Larry David/Jerry Seinfeld sort of way, and heartbreaking, too. But I'm proud of him. He's putting together the pieces of his completely upended life, getting a hold on the whole thing, and steadily loosening the grip his grief has had on him.

"Cuy," I say, "You know what I think? I think God is bigger than all the religions humans have put in place. He's no religion and He's all religions."

"So He's like Switzerland," my sweet son interjects, chomping on a piece of steak that, miraculously, meets his exacting standards. "You know, neutral."

"If that helps you, then yes, God is like Switzerland. And when people die, He doesn't consider what color they were, or what church they went to. He just looks deep inside their heart and he knows, in an instant, if they were genuinely good. And if they were good, they go to Heaven—"

"And if not, they go to Hell," Cuy responds, finishing the sentence for me. "Dad was good," he says quietly, color filling his freckled cheeks.

"Very good," I nod.

"He deserved to go to Heaven. It's Cancer that deserves to go to Hell."

I swear he's going to cry, and then suddenly he brightens.

"You think maybe diseases go to Hell?" He asks. "Like smallpox and polio and the plague. They deserve to go. And Cancer;

Cancer deserves its own section. What do you think? You think it's possible?"

Hell if I know, hon, but I sure do hope so.

Mommy/Daddy Houses Need Not Apply

We had a couple of hours to kill before the New York Giants game one Sunday, so I took the boys to look at houses. Not because we have to move, we don't. Our five-hundred-acre farm is owned by family, so we can stay as long as we like or at least until I get fed up with finding long black snakes curled up in the kitchen sink and escaped cows eating buttered popcorn off the back seat of the Mustang,

If I may digress for just a moment, and because you might be wondering what the heck I'm talking about, the cows were free to nosh because, like an idiot, I left the top down after a trip to the movies and the kids, of course, left a mess. As for the snakes in the sink? It's par for the course where we live and, at this point, I could care less. I get the salad tongs, grab the snake, plop it in a pot, slap on the top, and take it outside. Then I throw the pot and the tongs in the trash, and do a little "Woo-hoo, I get to go to Wal-Mart!" dance.

Hey, it's Wal-Mart. It's not like I'm throwing out stuff from Williams Sonoma.

In any case, I took the kids to look at houses not because we're tired of the cows or the snakes or the spooked polo ponies that occasionally run up onto our front porch, do a few laps, and then dart back off in the direction of whatever spooked them in the first place, but because the three of us miss people. Cuyler wants to be able to call for his friends. Casey wants to be within walking distance of work. And I'd be lying if I didn't admit that this place is just too isolated for me. I miss crowds, shopping, and overpriced coffee. Oh, and sidewalks. I so miss sidewalks! Even with their ankle turning unevenness and deep, heel snapping cracks, they're better than getting caught in a cattle guard any day.

Of course everyone and their brother advised me not to make any major changes in the year following Stu's death. My mom said, "Don't move." My girlfriends said, "Don't take the boys away from their friends." Ellen said, "Don't push yourself to start another book."

It might have been nice if somebody had said, "Don't get bangs" but they didn't. And if you can't make good a decision about something as simple as hair, you've got no business looking at houses.

But look we did. Me in my bangs. My boys in their Giants caps. And the more we looked the louder a voice in my head screamed, "You need a husband to live here! You see that light, the one hanging from the vaulted ceiling in the entry foyer? You're gonna need a twenty-foot ladder to change the bulb when it blows. You can't lug a twenty-foot ladder, Susan, and you can't climb a twenty-foot ladder. You're petrified of heights! Every time it needs to be changed, it's gonna cost you a hundred bucks to hire a handyman to come do it. You don't have a hundred bucks to piss away on handymen. You need it for haircuts. Because God knows, you've got to do something about these bangs!"

By the time we got home I had a migraine, a stomachache, and two kids who wanted to know why I kept tugging at my hair. It didn't look like the G-men were going to make me feel any better, but suddenly they rallied and won. And then a real miracle occurred.

"Mom," Casey started, "we know it's not our decision–"

"But those were 'mom and dad' houses." Cuyler said, cutting him off.

I looked from one son to the other and frankly, I saw dollar signs. *I've given birth to men who read minds! Sure, it took a long time to kick in, but just think of how many toilets I — and millions of other women — won't fall into in the future!*

"Seriously, mom," continued Casey, interrupting my reverie (and my plans to call the people at the Guinness Book of World Records), "all of those houses are 'old' us."

"We need 'new' us," offered Cuyler, "a whole new adventure." He paused. "Maybe, like, an apartment?"

"An apartment?" I asked, barely able to mask my joy at the mere mention of the same idea I'd had several times earlier in the day but was too scared to suggest. "You want to go from five hundred acres to eleven hundred square feet and a front stoop?"

They nodded.

You know, maybe bangs weren't such a bad call after all.

How Better to Hide the Blood?

I'm out on our front lawn finally dealing with Stu's rotted pear tree. The bees that have taken over like squatters in an abandoned building are none too happy to see me, and in a frantic, spastic moment of ducking, swiping, swearing, and begging God not to let me get stung, I step on a swollen, decomposing pear bursting with dozens of them.

Instantly they swarm my foot. For old, improperly shod Susan, (read: platform wedges while feeding the chickens), this would've meant immediate agony and maybe the use of an Epi pen. Ok, that's an exaggeration. I have no idea if I have a bee allergy. I've never been stung. But I do know that it would hurt like hell and if I didn't die, I'd probably want to or else, in my infinite agony, I might really go around the bend and kill my kids for being in front of the TV playing video games instead of out here helping me like I asked them to. Or maybe I'd just finally come to my senses and toss all that stuff in the trash.

Hmm. Maybe a bee sting is the way to go.

In any case, I step and connect with a bloated, oozing pear the bees are gorging themselves on, and they in turn connect with my foot. My work-boot-clad-foot. That's right, after years of living on a farm in nothing but high heels (and the rest of my clothing, of course; I had to stop farming naked when the cattle complained), I'm finally wearing the appropriate footwear.

Why? Because recently I learned the hard way that platform wedges and all manner of open-toed sexiness look, well, sexier, if the toes peeping out aren't purple and blue and bleeding through a mountain of bandages.

To be clear, not all my toes were purple and blue and bleeding through a mountain of bandages. Just the main toe, the most crucial toe, particularly as it pertains to balance, mobility, and, most importantly, pedicures. Yes, I'm talking about the showcase toe. The VIP of the peep-toed pump toe. The toe that, as it turns out, bleeds like a head wound when hit by a hatch door. Yes, the big toe.

How did I come to this hard-won discovery? Well frankly it came to me late one night on a sailboat with some friends.

I hopped up to be helpful (never a good sign as I sail with about as much proficiency as I farm) and offered to drop the anchor. If you're wondering what misguided notion possessed me to make such an offer well, it's simple. It'd done it One Whole Time Before, and there was wine involved. And in my happy, fuzzy mind, that combination practically qualified me to be Captain.

Now at least on the farm, I'd have been wearing shoes. The wrong shoes, but shoes, nonetheless. On the boat, I was barefoot. I was also wearing a very cute bathing suit that, sadly, will never see the Chesapeake Bay or any body of water ever again. Sky blue with spring green swirls of color, it was my favorite right up until the moment splatters of blood rendered it something Carrie might have worn to the after-prom pool party.

What can I say? I'm old, and even in searing pain I can still recall the days when "Carrie" was the benchmark for horror films. Which is sort of what the scene resembled when the hatch door took out my toe.

I have a vague recollection of flying into Little Miss Misguided Enthusiasm mode, announcing "I'll help with the anchor!" and racing to the bow of the boat. (The bow, for you landlubbers like me, is the front of the boat. But this really isn't about how much sailing lingo I've learned, is it?) Then I threw open the hatch, stomped on the anchor release button, and howled like the epidural quit mid push as the heavy metal door came crashing down onto the big toe on my right foot, an extremity already so hideous, it looks more like a disfigured hamster than a human body part.

Three weeks after my debacle, I'm still hobbling along on a toe that's swollen and sore and nearly devoid of its nail, but I've learned my lesson. From now on, it's work boots on the farm (take that, bees!), and deck shoes on a boat. In fact I plan to break in my new pair the next time I go sailing – but I've no plans to bring a bathing suit.

After all, I'm still me. All misguided enthusiasm and helpfulness. And for that reason alone I'm going with jeans, black jeans. Because really, how better to hide the blood?

****

****

Top 3 Things I've Learned in the Last 5 Days ...

3. Popping out a painfully dry, cloudy contact lens while driving is a virtually surefire way to lose the lens. And doing it while turning the AC on full blast guarantees you'll do the rest of your errands half blind. At least until you stop, spend ten minutes combing the stunningly filthy car floor, find the folded, hairy, crumb covered lens, suck it back to life, and pop it in your eye.

2. Tearing out a clump of hair and a couple of eyelashes during a therapy session devoted to the topic of your trichotillomania (a.k.a. compulsive hair pulling which began before your husband got sick and reached new heights after he passed), will result in your psychiatrist making you spend the remaining forty-five minutes wearing a hand puppet. Specifically, a bumble bee hand puppet. It was cute, but it clashed with my outfit.

1. Just because you're driving through town and your younger son spies Moser Funeral Home and shouts, "Hey! Isn't that where we had Dad serviced?" and your older son replies, "Shoulda had his oil changed too!" is no reason to drive off the road. Unless of course you've lost a contact lens or been forced to leave your cool bumble bee hand puppet at the psychiatrist's office so other budding baldies can use it.

****

****

A Question of Cancer

Cuyler is leaning in the doorway watching me make my bed. For a moment I consider turning on the mom charm and saying, "Don't just stand there, young man. Get in here and help me!" but the fact is, I don't need help making half a bed. Since Stu's death, I sleep only on what used to be his side of our king size bed. It makes me feel a little closer to him, and a lot closer to the Louisville Slugger tucked next to his nightstand.

In any case, it takes all of three seconds to fluff the pillow, straighten the sheets, and smooth the comforter. When I'm done, I look in my son's direction.

"What's up, dude?"

There's a pause, and then my budding heartbreaker with the broken heart and newfound knack for asking me things I wish he wouldn't even think about, looks me right in the eye and lobs his latest killer query.

"What's going to happen to me and Casey when you get cancer?"

Excuse me? Did I miss a memo? Or maybe another proclamation from the Mayans?

"I'm not going to get cancer," I respond immediately, without thinking, once again letting the gumball machine that masquerades as my mouth get away from me.

He shoots me a look, then flings himself onto the center of the bed I just finished making. "You don't know that" he says, his voice tight. "Dad didn't know he was going to get cancer. But he did. And he died. What happens to us if you die?"

"But I'm not going to die," I reply, grabbing his ankles, pulling him toward me, and tickling him behind both knees. "Though I might kill you for the mess you're making of my comforter!"

To be honest, I could care less about the bed and the only thing I'd like to kill is the cancer that wasn't content just to take my kids' dad. It had to take their peace of mind, too.

Casey fares a bit better. To a degree, his autism has acted as a bubble, protecting him, and softening his pain. He has his moments, but because he has the most amazing memory I've ever seen, it's a little easier to comfort him. "Quick," I say, when he's crying because he dreamt about Stu and awakened to the gut-wrenching reality that it was, sadly, just a dream, "tell me your top three Dad stories from our first summer on the farm!" In an instant, he's recounting things I haven't thought of in years. (Like the day Stu discovered a black snake napping next to him in his hammock. Did he flip? You bet. The damn thing had also been in his beer.) In almost no time Casey's off and running full tilt down memory lane and I'm asking God for patience because Cuy and I are in for a really long day of Dad tales.

But Cuyler is a different story altogether. He's always been one of these people who thinks a lot (clearly not a trait he inherited from his mother), but since Stu's death he's become a champion brooder. Some days are better than others, but on those other, awful days, he's like an open wound. His grief and pain, fear and worry about the future are palpable. I want to hug him, but he wants none of it. I remind him I'm here if he wants to talk, and then I do the only thing I can do. I back off. And wait. And eventually he comes around with a question or a statement that makes my head spin.

"Mom, be serious for a second!" He breaks my grasp and lunges for one of the huge decorative pillows I keep on the bed. "I'm not kidding," he shouts, trying not to laugh. "Answer me, or I'm throwing this stupid thing to Tug!"

He holds the pillow over the edge of the bed and Tug, the beautiful but intellectually challenged pup he adores practically passes out with excitement.

"Cuy," I say, looking from my son to my pillow to the dog, who's so excited, he's drooling like a waterfall all over the floor, "I'm healthy. I take vitamins and," I continue, warming to my pitch and knowing he's going to freak out when I finish, "I'm still young!"

"You're fifty!" he fires back. "You're practically at death's door!"

You know, maybe I did miss a memo. But I didn't miss the split-second opportunity to leap, snatch the pillow, and pin my kid to the bed in one fell swoop.

At death's door my butt.

"So here's how it lays out, oh master worrier," I offer, taking a break from tickling him. "If I get cancer, or struck by lightning, or if I break my neck trying to keep one of my favorite decorative accessories away from your dumb dog, you guys will go live with Aunt Nancy and Uncle Doug, or Uncle Nick. Ok?"

"What about Uncle Dan?"

"Uncle Dan already has four kids."

"And a Camaro." He smiles.

"Oh, so it's ok if I die as long as you go to the family member with the coolest car?"

He laughs a little and looks away, his eyes filled with tears.

"Listen Cuy," I sigh, hugging him, "I can't promise you that nothing's going to happen to me. But I can promise you there's a plan if something does. You'll be loved, and taken care of, and go to college, and do all the things you want to do. Unfortunately, there's no provision for a Camaro, but I think I could swing a king size bed. Any interest?"

"It's kind of a mess," he responds, giving me the sweetest smile, "and I don't want those big pillows, but maybe." Then he hops down, steps toward the door, and stops. "Whoops! Sorry," he says, spinning around. "I meant to help you make it."

And I didn't even have to turn on the mom charm.

****

TO: Friends and Family

FR: Susan

SUBJECT: Clearly I didn't get cards in the mail. . .

But I want you to know we're thinking of you.
> 'Twas two days before Christmas, and all through this place
>> Presents are hidden in every weird space.
>> Boxes tucked in cabinets, bags under the sink.
> Will my guys seek them out there? They're men, what do you think?
>> Some hiding spots are so good, all I can say,
>> Is, "I hope I recall them after a little Chardonnay."
>> 'Cause it'll only be me, late Christmas Eve night
> Putting gifts under the tree, while my young men sleep tight.
> With my wine glass and my flashlight, and my longshoreman's mouth
> Saying, "How the f--k could I lose stuff in such a small house?"
>> Eventually I'll get done, and go up to bed
>> And discover my pillow, tucked under Tug's head.
>> He misses Stu terribly, and he's not alone
> (Oh crap, someone help me, where'd I put his new bone?)
> Our first holiday season as a threesome has been kinda tough,
>> But we're making it through thanks to you and your love.

It's two days before Christmas and I just want to say,
We love you. We're thinking of you. Have a very merry day!
Love,
Susan, Casey, and Cuyler

****

Farm (Mis)management 101

When you live on a farm, there are a few simple rules you need to know. Things like, when the power goes out fill the bathtub, if you open a gate, close it behind you even if whatever you're doing will only take a minute, keep the cattle guards clear, if you drive a convertible, make sure you put the top up at night and, if lightning strikes your haybales and they burst into flames, you've just been promoted to firefighter.

Beyond these rules, there are other things to bear in mind simply because, in my experience, they're true. For starters, cell phone service will always be spotty, and that's putting it mildly. The supermarket will be twenty or thirty minutes away, so for God's sake, don't forget anything while you're there. And when the fuel indicator in your car says you're down to a quarter of a tank, get thee to a gas station, stat.

Sadly, and as I'm certain it will come as no surprise, I've learned all these things the hard way.

I have indeed run out of gas, tried to call Triple A for assistance only to discover I had no service, left the top down on the Mustang only to be greeted by snakes sunbathing in the backseat the next morning, and gone to the store for milk and returned to discover I stocked up on everything but. I was also once briefly promoted to firefighter, though something about my screaming with panic forced Stu to fire me on the spot. Regarding the gates that are scattered throughout the property we're all pretty good about closing those we open and know that if we come upon one that's already open, to leave it that way.

It's keeping the cattle guards clear that messes us, ok me, up.

A cattle guard is a series of metal pipes laid across a ditch. If the cattle try and cross it, their feet slip between the pipes and they get stuck. There isn't a heifer in the whole world that wants to get caught like that, so it's a terrific deterrent. But to keep it working properly, you've got to keep the ditch from filling with debris. Sand, gravel, dirt, leaves, tree branches, when stuff like that gets in the ditch, it renders it useless and before you know it you've got cows in the backyard, visiting the neighbors, and strolling around in the street.

Not good.

The other thing that can render a cattleguard useless is snow and ice. And while I'm pretty good about keeping it clear when it's warm out, it doesn't even cross my mind when it's cold. I don't want to be cold and I don't want to deal with anything that requires me to go out into the cold. You know where this is headed, right?

I'm upstairs pulling on Stu's old, ratty Ridgewood Jr. Football sweatshirt because I'm freezing. It snowed and the temperature is, like, zero, and all I want is to curl up on the sofa and continue watching every single last episode of Friday Night Lights with Cuy when, speak of the devil, he appears at my bedroom door.

"We've got cattle out."

I'm not kidding when I tell you that for me, there are no four worse words on the planet except for, of course, "your husband has cancer" and "we're out of coffee."

"You guys leave a gate open?" I respond, surprised. They haven't done that in ages.

"No. The guard froze."

Shit.

I follow him down the stairs and pull on my jacket and gloves and sneakers. I don't own snow boots. Snow boots mean you're planning to go out in the snow, and I never plan to go out in the snow. I like my snow where I can see it, from a window with a piping hot cup of coffee in my hand.

"You think we need to ask Jeff to help?" I ask, referring to Cuy's friend who lives in the first house on the property. Wrangling cattle is easier with three people and Casey is away. He's at a special school learning to drive. He hates it. I hate that he hates it and I really hate that it looks like a sanitarium from the 1950s. I cried leaving him there but I promised myself while Stu was dying that when we came to the end of that marathon, I'd get back to kicking Casey's butt – in a good way. The way we always did. The way that made the three specialists who diagnosed him with autism when he was thirteen tell us, and I quote, "Whatever you're doing with your kid, keep doing it."

But I'm getting ahead of myself. I'll get back to Case shortly. Right now, there's cattle to wrangle.

"I think we can handle it," Cuy replies as we both step into the mudroom, Tug and Grundy hot on our heels, and discover six heifers hanging out near the picnic table and Adirondack chairs, and one so close to the screen door it looks like she's come to borrow a cup of sugar.

"What's the plan?" I ask, mentally preparing myself to be flat on my butt in thirty seconds not just because of my sneakers but because I'm certain Tug will trip me on my way out the door.

"I'll go stand by the guard," Cuy replies and then, nodding in the direction of our guest at the screen door, "You stay here and deal with Mrs. 'Pardon Me, Have You Any Grey Poupon?'"

What the–? "How do you know that commercial? You're too young to know that commercial!"

"Oh mama," he replies, smiling and stepping outside, the dogs shooting out alongside him, thank God, "I am wise beyond my years!"

The cattle pay no attention to my beautiful boy as he jogs up to the guard, about fifty yards from the house, his long hair the color of hot chocolate bursting out of his cap.

Ooooh. Hot chocolate.

"I'm ready!" he shouts.

Making a mental note to make us both hot chocolate when we're back in the house, I turn to Mrs. Poupon. "Time to go home, girlfriend."

I step outside, position myself between Mrs. P. and the door, assume the "I'm about to do jumping jacks" stance they teach in cattle farming 101, and stand as tall as I can. Cattle are height dominant and, even though Mrs. P. probably weighs seven-hundred pounds and could take me down in an instant, she, sweet thing, sees me as a force to be reckoned with and slowly starts turning in Cuy's direction. Some force. As she's turning, I'm slipping. I fumble for the handle on the door, connect, but go down anyway, nearly dislocating my shoulder in a fruitless effort to keep my freezing butt from connecting with the frozen ground.

Everything hurts but slowly and carefully, desperate not to slip again and promising God I'll get snow boots, I stand up and begin limping in the direction of the cattle who are still lollygagging in our yard, munching on whatever frozen grass is poking out beneath the snow and ice. "Let's go, ladies," I say, making a sort of sweeping gesture with my outstretched arms. Cuy, positioned by the guard, is in the aforementioned jumping jack stance and ready to guide them back across it – easy enough to do because it is indeed filled with snow and frozen solid – or stop them should they try and veer off and take a stroll down the road. The dogs, on the other hand, are playing in the pasture we're moving the ladies into, most likely wet with snow and covered in whatever warm manure they can find. Lovely.

We've only been outside a few minutes but already my teeth are chattering. At least the girls are cooperating, I think, as they slowly head back into the pasture. They're so sweet and docile, and for a second I feel a little guilty for loving ribeye steak so much. But only for a second.

Mrs. P. is the last of the group to cross the guard and it dawns on me that now I need to put something there to keep them in. Move a car? That'll mean driving in the snow. Tie a rope? Do we even have rope? Chains. We must have chains. Do we have chains?

I turn to ask Cuy what he thinks and he's laughing.

"What?" I ask.

"You really stuck your landing back there," he laughs. "Even the German judge gave you a ten."

Damn kid. "When are you going to get nearsighted like the rest of us?" I reply.

"I guess you don't want me to move the truck here, right?"

"Perfect eyesight and you read minds, impressive. No. You're not moving the truck and I'm not moving the truck. Daddy must have rope or chains or something around here that we can use."

A quick note about the truck: the truck – a beast of a pickup, an enormous, silver Dodge RAM – belongs to the farm, and the farm belongs to Stu's older brother, Doug. The thought of skidding on the ice and denting or scratching the truck and having to tell him – which would require the additional confession of my not having thought to block the cattle guard when it started snowing – was not something I relished the idea of doing. The poor man was already well aware of my dearth of farm management skills. Why make it worse?

In the end, the rope we found wasn't long enough and, if there were chains anywhere, we were too frozen to find them, so we did what any former suburbanites would do. We lined the chairs from our patio set across the guard and placed the two Adirondacks on each end for a little reinforcement. It looked ridiculous but it did the trick. And the dogs enjoyed sitting in them.

We were on the mud porch pulling off our jackets and gloves when Cuy offered to go fire up Friday Night Lights.

"Perfect," I replied. "I'll make us hot chocolate."

A few minutes later I was in the den, my happy, orange TJ Maxx mug in one hand, and Cuy's Redcoat-meets-Sgt.-Pepper creation in the other.

"We have milk!" Cuy exclaimed as I placed his hot chocolate on the ottoman.

"And cows in their proper place!" I replied with equal enthusiasm.

Careful not to step on Grundy-the-throw-rug in his favorite spot in front of the sofa, I plopped myself down next to Tug who was curled up next to Cuy and sniffed.

"Did you rinse them off," I ask.

"No way, mom! They were practically frozen!"

"Well they're defrosting and starting to stink," I reply, giving him the mom-eye.

He clicks the remote and the television screen fills with the opening montage of our favorite characters in fictional Dillon, Texas. Saracen taking care of his grandma. Coach Taylor solemnly walking the football field. Riggins passed out on the couch, empty bottles of beer cluttering the coffee table. I love this show, these characters, the writing. I stick my nose in my hot chocolate to block the dog stink. I should make Cuy wash them off right now but decide I can suffer through one episode.

And then the power goes out.

We wait, but nothing. Not even a flicker.

"Might as well wash the dogs," I say.

"But it's cold," Cuy whines in response.

"Then at least go fill the tub, ok?"

He nods, hops off the sofa, and heads for the stairs. Tug and Grundy, always up for an adventure, follow him. And it hits me.

"Cuy," I call. "While you're up there, wash the dogs."

"Really?"

"Yep!"

"Awesome!" he exclaims.

Yes, the bathroom was a complete disaster, but the dogs smelled better and, more importantly, we didn't forget to fill the tub. That's the rule and we followed it. And in my defense, it doesn't specify what you have to do with the water.

The Worst Mom in the History of Motherhood

As I mentioned, Casey was away at school the day the cattle guard froze. I call it school but it's really not. It's a rehabilitation center, a place that does life-changing things for the people who go there. And the people who go there, God bless them, have suffered strokes and brain injuries, and survived debilitating illnesses and car accidents. They've endured physical traumas that require learning a new job because they can no longer do their old one, or learning to drive a specially outfitted vehicle, or, in Casey's case, simply learning to drive.

Like I said, the place itself is as ugly as hell. The first time we went I wanted to cry when I saw it. *I can't leave him here,* I thought. *It looks like a sanitarium. It looks mean and cold and scary.* It was just so unfair; Casey's friends were touring college campuses and he was touring a rundown rehab facility. Ok, I lied at the top of this paragraph. I didn't want to cry, I did cry, in truth I sobbed in the ladies' room while we waited for the tour to begin.

I didn't make the decision to pursue this path alone though; Stu, Casey, and I, with the help of the department of aging and rehabilitative services, made it a few months before Stu's death. He and I knew with absolute certainty that, in the right environment and with instructors trained to work with people like Case, who have special needs that require maturity and patience and repetition to make the task at hand stick, he would get his driver's license and it would be as it is for all of us – the ticket to independence. The ticket to independence we were told he'd never have.

When Casey was 13, we took him to the University of North Carolina's Institute for Child Development. For a day and a half, a group of doctors, psychologists, and educators conducted a variety of tests and evaluations. They were terrific with Casey and us; patient, encouraging, and supportive. They also had a sense of humor, thank God, or else this mom might've had a not so social call from Social Services.

"Can you name a red flower?" the evaluator asked Casey as Stu and I watched through a one-way mirror.

"A rose," our son responded.

Stu and I high fived. *Way to go, Casey!*

"Good. Now, how about a cold food?" he continued.

"Ice cream," Casey replied.

Stu and I elbowed each other in the ribs. "He is so your son," I teased.

"Great," the evaluator said, smiling. "Just one last question and we're done for the day, ok?"

Casey nodded.

"Can you name a white drink?"

Together, Stu and I, along with the assistant sitting with us, whispered the word "milk" at the exact moment Casey shouted, "Wine!" And then added, as the evaluator cracked up, the assistant and Stu got hysterical, and I tried to hide, "My mom loves white wine!"

They mean well, these specialists, and those who've seen hundreds even thousands of people with autism can and frequently do give excellent advice. But they don't really know your kid, and they certainly don't know you. When they gave us Casey's official diagnosis of high functioning autism, they said he'd never drive, go to college, hold a job, or live on his own. He would be our "forever child."

To which Stu responded, "Screw that."

Screw that was our basic mentality when it came to Case and we'd embraced it long before his diagnosis. That bit of information didn't come until he was almost in high school and up until then, frankly? We just thought he was a little. . . different.

He'd flip out at birthday parties, panic when the lights went off in a movie theater, refuse to stand under the shower, and put his hands over his ears and cry if we had the music up too loud. What did we do when these (and other) things happened? We parented him. Took him home from the birthday party and explained that if he couldn't behave, he couldn't stay. Cajoled him until the movie started and the theater flooded with light. Stayed with him when he showered and occasionally got in with him. And when the music was too loud, sometimes we told him to suck it up and deal – it was the Beach Boys, for Pete's sake; who lowers the volume on the Beach Boys? – and sometimes we lowered it because, well, it wasn't the

Beach Boys. We treated Case like he was a regular kid, neurotypical as they say, because we didn't know he wasn't.

He played basketball and baseball and football and, because we knew there was something up we just didn't know what, Stu helped out with the junior football team to make sure Casey got time on the field – to do well and to take his lumps – just like all the other kids. And, when Stu became one of the program's official coaches, he hand-picked players based upon their parents and, in so doing, gave Casey a tightknit group of friends who had his back and still do today. Yes, by that point we were getting a clue that he might have a "thing," we just figured we'd continue handling it our way and, despite living in New Jersey which is considered the autism capital of the country, no one there ever suggested that getting him tested for such might be a good idea.

Leaving him at the Woodrow Wilson Rehabilitation Center was one of the most difficult things I've ever had to do. As we walked the halls, peeked into classrooms, and got him settled in his dorm room, he cried and begged me not to leave him there. And considering that I expected to discover an iron lung or electroshock chamber every time I turned the corner, I almost didn't.

I have to say though that the people were professional and nice. Really nice. Almost like they knew the place lacked in the ambience department and were trying super hard to compensate. They were cheerful and helpful and knew exactly how to distract him when it was time for me to leave. Our last stop was the cafeteria, and when he saw the selection, he kissed me and said "See ya!"

I cried the entire ride back to the farm. I prayed the place would indeed be his ticket to independence and I prayed he'd stay the course and not run away.

He'd run away before when we first moved to the farm. Just took off running up Rokeby Road toward Route 50. A neighbor who we didn't know (it's tough to know your neighbors when they're so far away you can't just stroll over to say hello unless you pack a lunch), stopped him and said, "Hey buddy, how 'bout you let me bring you home?" He did indeed bring my Casey home and all these years and so much more knowledge and information later, I know without a doubt that if we knew Case had autism – and all it entails –

prior to our move to the farm? We'd never have moved. We'd never have broken his heart like we did. Never have ripped him from his comfort zone, his friends, his routine.

Hell, we didn't even know to set his room up exactly as it had been in New Jersey – and when you move a child with autism that is the FIRST rule of thumb. Recreate their environment. The sameness gives them a sense of safety and security. All parents want their kids to feel safe and secure. We did too. But we didn't know.

And having said that and knowing how hard we worked – in the dark – to treat Case like a regular kid, I can't help thinking about the flip side. Stu was tough. He was a Marine. And as I know I've said, he called the shots. Maybe we would have moved anyway and wouldn't have made the move that easy. Maybe, on purpose, we'd have decided to move like most families do: you get to the new house, pick your room, and decorate it. Stu would never have appreciated or understood an "advance team" of decorators (me) getting my mitts on Casey's new room and setting it up exactly like the one in our home in Ridgewood. In fact, I can almost hear him saying, "Susan A., who's going to coddle him when you're dead?"

He'd have been right, of course, but still, when I think back, knowing all I do today, it breaks my heart to know we broke our son's to a million little pieces and we didn't even realize it.

And so, I left him at Woodrow. And he was there just four days when the phone call came.

It was his counselor, and she wanted me to know that he wanted to go home. Me too, I thought, flashing on my mom's house and her full fridge and how I can put on ten pounds just peeking inside. I know that sounds flip, but I was tired. I was at work. And I don't mean mismanaging the farm work. I had to get a job, and by golly, I got one. And I was brand new and trying desperately to make the lovely people who hired me happy they did.

"Mrs. McCorkindale," she continued, "he's insisting."

He's insisting? I thought. *He's basically a twelve-year-old trapped in the body of a twenty-year-old and he's at your particular school to, please God, learn to drive so someday he can take a girl out without needing me to tag along and you're listening to him?*

"I'm sure he is," I said. I know Case would much rather be home, lying on his bed and listening to music or eating crap and playing Call of Duty: Modern Warfare 300 for six hours at a clip than go to class. Heck, I don't know a single one of his friends who wouldn't. But I can't just cave and come get him. He needs to do this, all my concerns about iron lungs lurking in dark corners aside.

"Mrs. McCorkindale," she whispered, "I'm really concerned about him."

"Thank you," I said. "I appreciate that. My guess is he's sitting there, across your desk, telling you he can't eat, can't sleep, and has a headache, right? He's hunched over, head in hand, sniffling, and frankly he looks like his dog just up and died, his best friend ditched him or, worse yet, his cell phone fell in the toilet. That sound about right?"

"A hundred percent."

I have to laugh. Casey's not away a week, and already he's at DefCon 4 on the drama king scale. Clearly there are no delays in his mastery of manipulation.

"Might I speak with him for a moment?" I ask.

I hear some shuffling and then my gentle giant's sweet, flat monotone. "Mom," he says, sobbing, "I want to come home. Everyone here is weird."

I want to say *I know, baby, I know. I know you stick out like a sore thumb because all your parts are intact.* I want to say *Knock it off, you're there to learn to drive, not because your life's been upended by some horrific illness or accident.* I want to say *Be grateful because you're healthy and because so many people converged to give you this opportunity, so many people believe in you.* I want to say, *Stu, God damn it, where are you? I feel like I spend every moment of the day trying to keep my balance in a moon bounce!* But I don't say any of it. I can't. I have to be bad cop and good cop without losing my cool.

"Casey," I say, "there are weird people everywhere, normal people, too. Only you won't get to meet any of them if you don't get a driver's license."

"But I want to come home."

"And I want Robert Downey, Jr. to show up at the door."

"Mom," he says softly, "you're being silly."

"No, you're being silly. You want to come home? Start walking."

"But mom, please—"

Taking a breath the size of our beast of a pickup and praying to God I'm doing the right thing, I cut him off.

"Not a chance, dude. You want out? Lace up your sneakers, grab your backpack and a couple of bottles of water. I figure it should take you three days to get home, two if your cell dies and you can't text me every ten seconds begging and pleading for me to pick you up."

"But mom, that's dangerous!"

"Double the reason you should stay put and do what you told Dad you'd do."

Silence. A really long silence during which I could tell he'd stopped crying and was, I hoped, recalling the conversation he had with me and Stu just a few weeks before the cancer and the chemo and the powerful narcotic pain medication combined to completely destroy Stu's ability to communicate in any rational manner. I didn't want to play the Dad card, but sometimes you've got to invoke the dead to guilt the living into submission. And besides, I was starting to waiver. My stomach was screaming *Stand up from this desk and go get your child! He needs you. He's scared. This isn't working. Go. Get. Him!*

"Ok," he finally said. "I'll stay."

Funny thing is, I expected the call to come much sooner. You know, like within the first twenty-four hours and frankly, I was proud of him for lasting as long as he did.

"Hey Case," I said, as we were hanging up, "I love you. Dad loves you, too. He always believed in you, baby. Do this, and let's stick it to those stupid specialists."

"I will, mom, I promise," he said.

And three days later he strolled into the house, having made his escape from the rehab facility with the help of a friend.

****

"He called me and said they were weird and mean to him," MJ said.

I look from MJ to Casey. We're standing in the hall near the front door that's still held together with duct tape, and poor MJ looks very surprised to see me looking very surprised. Not to mention angry.

"Mom! Please! Don't be mad! You don't know what it was like there!"

I look back at MJ like, *and?*

"And he said you were super busy and that it was ok with you if he came home." MJ's sputtering and looking at Case like *How could you do this to me, dude?* which is cool with me because I'm thinking the same thing. *How could you do this, Case? All the effort that went into arranging this opportunity, plus your promises to your dad and me to stick it out. How could you do this?* "He said you didn't have time to go get him, so I went and got him."

I can't speak, not something that happens to me too frequently.

"I guess I should have called you first to make sure," MJ stammers.

MJ taught a few of the vocational classes at the high school, and that's where he and Casey became friends. Case thinks MJ is awesome and he is. He's great to my son; drives all the way out to the farm to shoot hoops or take Case to bowling or movie nights with his church youth group. He is mature and polite and responsible. When Case is with MJ, I know he's in good hands and I don't worry.

But yes, he should have called me.

"Case," I finally say, "I'm giving your allowance to MJ."

"What? Why? No fair!" he shouts, dropping his backpack to the floor with such a crash I'm sure he's cracked one of the wooden planks.

"And MJ, I'm giving you Casey's allowance because yes, you should have called me and now *you* are going to finish teaching him to drive and *you* are going to get him through the written test."

"Computer," Casey snaps. "You take it on the computer."

"Forgive me," I say. "MJ, I'm going to give you Casey's allowance because you should have called me and now you're going to finish teaching him to drive and you're going to get him through the *computerized* test."

I pause to enjoy watching MJ's head bob up and down and Casey slump against the wall like he's just been sentenced to life in prison without video games.

"I'll also pay you for gas," I add, "but you two are finishing this and it's not finished until he passes that test. Got it?"

MJ nods. Casey rolls his eyes. "You're so mean to me, mom," he says. "You'd never do this to Cuy!"

"You're right," I reply. "I'm a terrible mom. The worst in the history of motherhood. Now you two work out the details."

I turn to walk away and stop.

"MJ," I say, "thanks for going to get him and bringing him home safely."

He smiles and shrugs, and we both look at Case, who's sitting cross-legged on the floor. He's got his face in his hands, so I take the opportunity to pretend to shoot myself in the head. This gives both of us the giggles, and Case's head pops up so fast he whacks it into the wall.

"Dammit!" he shouts. "Look what you made me do!"

Of course, it's my fault; everything is my fault.

"What's so funny?" he asks, scowling at me.

"Almost everything," I reply, still laughing, "if you look at it in the right light."

****

"You want me to drive?" I tease, opening the door to the Durango and smiling at Casey, who's already buckled up behind the wheel.

He responds with his trademark eye roll, so I hop in. "Just kidding," I offer.

No reply. He starts the car, checks his seatbelt, and adjusts the rearview mirror. I turn up the heat. It's cold, and I'm nervous, which is making me colder.

"You want music?" I ask, reaching for the dial on the radio.

"No!" he barks. "I have to concentrate!"

"Ok, sweetheart," I say. "Sorry. Don't be nervous."

"I'm not nervous!"

He checks both side mirrors, puts the car into reverse, and then so slowly you'd think we were backing out of a parking spot at Target at the height of the Christmas shopping season, begins to back the car out of the driveway and down our dirt road. It's been about ten minutes and we've gone maybe a hundred yards. At this rate it will take us an hour to get to the DMV, which is 20-minutes from our house.

I glance at my boy who's concentrating so hard I can see the muscles bulging in his neck and close my eyes. Not because I'm worried he's going to kill the both of us, but because I can feel tears welling up; Stu, I think, he's doing it. Can you see him? Are you watching this? Our son, the one we were told would do so little in his life, is proving those doctors wrong in real time, baby. I wish you were here. I wish you were taking him today. You kicked his ass so hard sometimes, he hated you, but under all that Marine-style tough love, you were a mush; you were his greatest champion. You done good, Stu. I hope you're watching. He's going to pass this test, sweetheart, and then he's going to be like every other kid on the planet – constantly asking for gas money.

At that I laughed out loud and Case shot me a quick glance.

"What's funny?" he asked. And then, "Why are you crying?"

"Just proud of you, sweetheart, and thinking how proud Dad would be if he could see you."

And then, without taking his eyes off the road, the kid those doctors discounted said simply, "He can see me, mom. And this isn't all he's going to watch me do."

****

We got to the DMV, went in, and by some stroke of luck, Casey was at the computer and taking the test within five minutes.

He passed on the first try.

Then he left for the driving portion and I stood at the window watching for his return. It felt like forever, and then, after I'd reminded myself to breathe about three hundred times, I saw our fire engine red Durango come down Blackwell Road. I saw the left turn signal come on, and the car slow as he turned into the parking lot. At that moment, I knew he passed. A minute later he walked in with the woman who'd taken him for the test. She was smiling.

"He's drives a little slow, but that's ok, Mrs. McCorkindale," she said.

"He passed?" I replied, trying not to cry.

"He passed," she replied.

And then my big son, my baby, swooped me up in his long arms as I burst into tears and said, "Thank you, mom."

"No, Case," I replied, "You did it. You did the work. You can do anything."

"That's what Dad always said."

And he was right.

Bounce Boost

Not long after Casey got his license, I was asked to address a group of retired teachers about what it's like to raise a child with autism. My first thought was, "It's the toughest job you'll ever love." My second thought was, who's slogan was that?

As it turns out it was the Peace Corps, and the ad read: We need someone with a good back, strong stomach, level head, and a big heart. Peace Corps. The Toughest Job You'll Ever Love.

They might as well have been advertising for autism moms or, more specifically, autism parents. We fit every aspect of that job description and love our "work" more than we love breathing.

But it's not an easy road, by any means.

The day the three smart, well-meaning doctors gave us Casey's diagnosis, I wanted to cry. Hearing them say he'd never drive, live on his own, hold a job, or manage his own money, broke my heart. I didn't cry though, and Stu was stone cold silent.

Until we left the building.

"Screw that," he spat.

A week or so later, in the kitchen one night after dinner, he asked me if I recalled a conversation we had when I was thinking of leaving my job to write full time. We were living in New Jersey, I was commuting to the city, and out of the clear blue sky I started picking up assignments.

"Sort of," I replied. "I'm not sure. We talked so much about that whole thing."

"Allow me to remind you," he said, patting the chair next to him for me to sit down. "You really wanted to make a go of it, but you kept saying, 'I don't think I have what it takes.'"

That I recalled, and I smiled because it was nice to be reminded I'd been wrong.

And then he continued.

"Those doctors last week?" he said, leaning in and squeezing my hand, "They don't think Casey has what it takes."

"I know," I replied, pinching my eyes tight to hold back my tears.

"Well," he said, "they're wrong. Just like you were wrong. They don't know our kid. They don't get to call those shots. We're his parents. We call the shots."

"Yes, but–"

"What if they're right? We'll find out for ourselves. But until then, we push."

I nodded yes.

"You have to trust me, Susan A., nobody is going to limit what our Casey can do."

And nobody did.

At this writing, Casey, the toughest job Stu and I ever loved, has the kind of independence all parents want for their children: he has his own apartment, a job he loves, pays his own bills, and is currently driving car number three, numbers one and two having been deemed not cool enough once he got really comfortable behind the wheel. He is independent because we – and he – didn't allow anyone or any opinion to limit him.

Only you can limit your success, your greatness. How far you go is up to you. Never allow anyone to put a cap on what you or someone you love can do.

Shoot for the moon, as the saying goes. Even if you miss, you'll land among the stars.

Too Much Time on My Hands. And Face.

I don't know what other people do when their life goes from beyond frenzied to normal, but I know that for me it opens a Pandora's box of opportunities to focus on myself – and not in a good way.

Since Stu's death, I've gone from pulling out my eyelashes (but not eating them, though I hear that's a thing) to yanking the greys out of my hair to trying to scratch the age spots off the backs of my hands. While I'm pleased to report that the bumble bee hand puppet helped me move on from these misguided activities, I must confess I have a brand-new fixation: my face.

My face is falling.

If I said this to you, in person, you'd probably laugh, like Trish did, and tell me not to be ridiculous. Or maybe you'd say, "Oh

Aunt Susan, you're so silly," like my eight year-old niece did when she caught me one Christmas Eve, trying to shove my sagging skin up into my hairline and hissing a desperate prayer to Santa to *please, please leave surgical clips in my stocking!*

He didn't of course, he utterly ignored me. My sweet niece, on the other hand, quickly wrapped one of her Dora the Explorer headbands and gave it to me Christmas Day saying, "This will pull it all back nice and tight!" Isn't she cute? Convincing, too. It didn't work, but that only means she's on her way to a major marketing career.

Honestly though, I'm not being silly or ridiculous. I'm stating a fact. My face is falling. It's getting loose and flabby. "Lax" as the facelift web sites say, particularly around my mouth where little puffs of skin have started to appear. They look like pouches and they'd be perfect for storing nuts for the winter if I were a squirrel which, as of this writing, I'm not, unless the fuzzy blonde mustache I've also sprouted means I'm on my way to whiskers and if that's the case then I really am going to cry.

And we all know that won't help, unless I'd like to store nuts in my eyelids, too.

Frankly, I feel lied to, tricked, baited and switched, double crossed, and conned. Why? Because everyone knows it's the neck that goes first, so that's what I've been watching. My neck! I was told that sooner than later my neck would cut and run. That it would wrinkle and sag. That the skin would bulge and flow in folds like lava down to my collar bone. That one morning I'd look in the mirror and discover a veritable Saint Bernard looking back. And then I'd have only one option: to break out the collection of silk scarves I've had in storage since the eighties and hope they hide the brandy barrel.

But it hasn't happened. My neck is fine. And I should know. I check it constantly. I've missed whole days and nights and special events because I was busy scrutinizing my neck. The once in a lifetime meteor shower everyone else watched? Missed it because it was neck check night. All those incredible Black Friday sales? Skipped them because I was staking out some possible skin tags. I feel so stupid. I've been completely preoccupied with my neck, when the whole time it's my face that's been up to no good.

Correction: down to no good. And no amount of pulling, smoothing, tugging, or trying to tuck it behind my ears is doing a damn thing.

"You need to do what my Grandma did," my favorite esthetician suggests one day when I'm in to see her for a facial and can't stop pulling at my squirrel pouches so she can confirm that, yes, sadly, I am on the road to rodent and from there it's just a hop, skip, and a sob before the great neck collapse and my arrival, crying and suffocating beneath immense folds of skin, at Saint Bernard-ville.

"You need a mini tuck."

She then went on to describe something about incisions near my ears and a whole lot of sucking fat and pulling skin and repositioning tissue and honestly, I don't know what else because I had to stop listening and run to the ladies' room where I stared in the salon's enormous mirror trying to decide what was making me sicker: my face, the thought of the only thing that might fix it, or the fact that an eighty-eight year-old Grandma can kick my butt in the guts department.

Good God, my butt. Yet another body part I could bellyache about all day. But I won't. This is, after all, about my face. And how I may never again bend over to pick up stray socks, collect dog hair, or dust the woodwork. Why? Because when I do, I can actually feel my skin plunging forward, slamming into the corners of my mouth, and forming what just might be the world's first face wattle.

Correction: the world's first *human* face wattle. Because it's not enough that I live on a 500-acre farm; I have to look like the livestock, too.

"You could try a clear, spray on adhesive," Cuyler suggests with a smirk when I make the mistake of telling him about my preoccupation with my face.

Excuse me?

"I think Dad kept some in the workshop," he continues, grinning. "You just tilt your head back, have your face fall where you want it, and spray it on along your hairline. I'll get it for you," he teases, reaching for the door. "But be careful; it's tacky for about three minutes until it dries, and you don't want feathers getting stuck in it."

Great. Then I'd really look like a rooster. Which is certainly better than a squirrel and a Saint Bernard, though not by much. But you know, I do kind of like the idea of an adhesive. Particularly if it works with the headband.

Taking My Lumps

It was about a week before the first anniversary of Stu's death at four-thirty in the morning and I was at my desk doing my best to crack myself up. I subscribe to the Mel Brooks school of humor which says, "If you laugh, they're going to laugh," so I always take my giggling – *if* I'm giggling – as a good sign and not the precursor to early onset dementia my sons insist it is.

Usually, the only parts of my body that move when I'm working are my fingers when I finally come up with something to say and start typing, and my head when I re-read what I've written and start pounding it against the keyboard.

(And now you know the real reason I wear bangs – they hide the bruises.)

On that particular morning, the dust on my screen was distracting me. I blew on it, but that didn't work. I cursed the woman who's supposed to clean the place and then laughed because, well, that's me and I've been on strike for quite some time. And then finally I just leaned in, like a lazy slob, and wiped it away with the sleeve of my sweatshirt.

And that's when I felt it. My right arm brushed my right breast and there it was: a nice, hard lump near my armpit. Such a discovery will undo you anytime. But if you happen to make such a find a mere seven days before the one-year anniversary of your husband's death from cancer, trust me when I tell you, you will flip out.

I certainly did.

I didn't know what to do first, so I did everything at once. I ripped off my sweatshirt, pulled my tee shirt over my head, and sent the following calm, collected, "I was a cancer caregiver, so I never lose my cool" text to two of my girlfriends. "OMG! Who's your doctor??? There's a lump in my breast the size of a malted milk ball!" Then, while frantically awaiting their replies which, since it was four-thirty in the morning took a while to arrive, I basically molested myself at my desk. This lasted about a minute and then, when poking at it with my finger didn't make the damn thing disappear, I raced to the bathroom where I stood half naked staring at myself in the mirror and mumbling, *Oh my God, I can see it. I can actually see it!*

Hmm, I thought briefly. *If this thing's adding to my spectacularly negligible cup size, who am I to complain?* And then I realized Case and Cuy are right; I really do have early onset dementia.

A short while later, having obtained the names of two doctors, one of whom is actually my doctor (I just forgot I had one in the midst of my panic attack) and having been talked in off the ledge by both girlfriends, my lump and I showered, dressed, and left for a job interview. A normal person would have cancelled and called the doctor for an appointment or shown up at the door and begged to be seen. But no, I soldiered on and spent sixty minutes trying not to say things like, "Yes, that was a highly successful program we did at *Family Circle* particularly since, at the time, I didn't have a lump the size of a butt cheek in my breast!"

Clearly, it's my flair for exaggeration and not dementia that will ultimately do me in.

Unless cancer gets me first.

Of course, that's all I could think about for the rest of the day.

At the hair salon: *Yes, please, pin straight, no product, and would you like to look at my lump?* And the supermarket: *A sale on fresh chicken breasts? So yours are acting up, too!* And on the sidelines at Cuy's flag football practice: *Monster catch, Cuyler! Now, who here wants to see something really scary?*

As I'm sure you can imagine I didn't sleep that night, but I did use the time productively.

I dug out my life insurance policy, re-read it, and cried because we'd finally have money and I wouldn't be around to spend it, put it with my will (to which I also attached a chapter from my book, *500 Acres and No Place to Hide* entitled "No Goody-bags at This Girl's Funeral" because while I do want food, drink and dancing at my repast, I draw the line at pretty velvet satchels filled with my cremains), and rearranged my shoe closet according to girlfriend:

- Rocking hot fur boots, Lisa T.
- Sophisticated Michael Kors pumps, Trish.
- Sexy little leopard print sling-backs, Lisa O.

- Pricey but painful Louboutin's, Sandra.
- Gorgeous, open-toed, sky-high Guess pumps, Jenn.
- Etc., etc.

I realize they won't fit any of my friends as none of us wears the same size I do, but still, it's the thought that counts. And I do want them thinking of me. After all, I'm the one with the lump the size of a Lear jet.

By mid-morning the next day I was finally, mercifully, sitting in the examining room waiting for my doctor (yes, the one I forgot I had but who you bet I remembered to call immediately after my job interview), when she comes breezing in all blonde and beautiful and business-like, asks how I am and I respond by ripping off my shirt.

"How am I? I think I'm dying, that's how I am. And it's so not fair. Stu's about to be gone a year and this," I reply, stabbing the damn lump which I swear has made the leap from Lear jet to Mauna Loa since the last time I checked, "is the anniversary gift I get! I'm petrified. That's how I am. My kids are going to wind up in foster care. Or worse. With family!"

She laughs and I'm a little relieved. Even at death's door I still kill. *And that'll be a twenty-five-dollar cover and a two-drink minimum. Here, let me stamp your hand.*

"Susan, it's probably just a swollen lymph node," she replied, examining me.

Huh. I hadn't thought of that. Ok, I had. But only for a sec. A swollen lymph node's easy, but I'm just not that lucky.

"I'm sending you for an ultrasound and maybe a mammogram. But only if the ultrasound is suspicious," she continued, "which it won't be. Ok?"

I wanted to ask her to pinky swear, do the whole "cross her heart hope to die, stick a needle in her eye" thing, but the needle bit screamed BIOPSY! so I stifled myself.

And then the real fun began.

I couldn't get an appointment for an ultrasound.

My local hospital had nothing open for the next ten days. Ten days! I could be dead by then! So I called this other hospital that I'd never even been to and begged. They gave me an appointment three days away, on Monday. That meant all I needed to do was get through Saturday and Sunday without inadvertently letting the kids know about my lump. Because if I slipped, they'd flip. They didn't need to be reminded what day it almost was, and they didn't need to worry about losing their mom while still mourning the loss of their dad.

I was practically paralyzed with fear, but not so paralyzed that I couldn't wield a wine glass.

And now you know how I spent the weekend. Drinking in the evening and barely able to put two words together in the morning. By Monday, not even hair like "Cousin It" could hide the damage I'd done to my forehead.

But alas, Monday did finally dawn. I jumped in the car with my bruises, what I was certain was a now Saturn-sized lump, and my doctor's orders for an ultrasound and a mammogram (maybe). I also brought directions to the hospital and called the nice people at OnStar as extra insurance to make sure I got there (and because I really get a kick out of trying to find someplace in Virginia with an assist from "Dave" in New Delhi).

I got lost anyway. I always do. I'm unsure what happens first when I'm in the car. The panic attack and then the realization that the sign I just passed shouldn't say "Welcome to West Virginia," or the sign followed by the panic attack followed by my pulling over on the side of the road crying and wondering if this time I really do need a rescue chopper.

Eventually though, I arrived, checked in, promised them my first-born male child should my health insurance refuse to cover me for some reason, and was ushered into a waiting room. Between getting lost and panicking, and having convinced myself that both didn't bode well, I was wrecked and really hoping to be alone with my lump. Not a chance. There were two older ladies already waiting and who greeted me with such sweet smiles and offers of bottled water, trail mix, tissues, and genuine concern that I just wanted to crawl into their laps. In short order we were talking, noshing, swilling, and sharing our respective reasons for being there.

Ok, they shared. I hesitated. Big mistake. They knew. They just knew. And then they wanted to know if my husband was waiting for me in the reception room.

"Um, yeah, no." I replied. "He died."

Stunned silence and then, "Bless your heart. And you didn't you bring a friend with you?"

Nah, I thought, shaking my head. *It's just me and Mauna Loa.*

"When did he die?"

"A year ago this week."

And then it was my turn to hand out tissues. *Great, Suz*, I thought. *Mel Brooks would not be pleased.*

Luckily, a couple of techs came along for the ladies and I picked up a copy of *Real Simple* which I really was trying to read when the lights went out. And came back on. And went out again. And then came on but only via generator which gave the room the same warm, comforting feeling one gets watching a slasher film.

That's when the camel's back broke. How many more signs did I need? I was done. God had spoken. I had my diagnosis. I was dying, and I was leaving. But not before going to the ladies' room.

Getting there was relatively easy. I followed the little grey lights glowing along the floor and bumped head on into a security guard who was none too pleased not to see me and who said, and I quote, "You really want to go in there? It's pitch black." And I was like, "Buddy, I'm a mom. You have no idea what we can do in the dark."

Just between you and me, I should've held it in, suffered, and scrammed. The bathroom was so dark I had to open the door a crack just to locate the toilet. I stood there with what little light there was streaming in, spied the commode and thought, *Ok Suz, your butt belongs over there.* And then I locked the door, turned, and strolled confidently into the sink. It took two more tries but I finally found the bowl, felt around for the toilet paper dispenser, put eight zillion strips all over the seat, and sat down.

Ah, sweet relief. But only until the instant I stood to pull up my underpants and caught my charm bracelet in the lace. *This can't be happening*, I thought, feeling the panic make a repeat appearance and the sweat stream down the back of my neck and into my hair. *Isn't it enough I'm dying, God?* I demanded. *You need to butcher my blow out, too?*

My brain raced. I couldn't see my hands in front of my face which was fine really as lifting my left one would've given me a wedgie and using both to reach down and grab my jeans just resulted in all kinds of unwanted southern exposure. I didn't know what to do so I stood there, bent over in the pitch black, practically naked and cursing my bracelet and my stupid boob. And then I heard the tech calling my name.

"Mrs. McCorkindale?" Pause. "Am I saying that correctly? Mrs. McCorkindale? Are you still here?"

"In here!" I yelled instantly, all fears of embarrassment and charges of indecent exposure evaporating. Hell, she's a medical professional. She's seen it all. What's one more half-naked woman? I hobbled in the direction of the door, opened it a bit and yelled, "Yes, I'm here! Help!"

Seconds later, by the light of the tech's cell phone, I freed myself from my Hanky Panky underpants, and just seconds after that I was on the table having Mauna Loa measured.

"It's amazing you can do this without power," I said.

"We have a generator," she replied, pressing the ultrasound wand hard and deep into my breast and armpit. "And you," she continued, pointing, clicking, and taking half a dozen images of my tiny ta-ta, "have a really swollen lymph node."

Then she got the radiologist who confirmed it wasn't cancer and I started to cry. It was so sweet because they both hugged me and gave me tissues and the tech offered me a bottle of water which cracked us both up. I thanked her again for quite literally saving my butt and walked out into the sunshine.

And then I drove home without getting lost which was good, because really? I'd taken enough lumps lately.

No 'Family Guy' at Grandma's

"I say we kill 'Julie'."

I throw my cell phone into my bag and turn to Cuyler, who's busy nudging the radio dial around with his nose. We're sitting in the car, waiting for his train to New Jersey that's almost three hours late, and "Julie," Amtrak's automated customer service "person," has just tacked on another fifteen minutes to the delay. At this point, my son's more than a little antsy and frankly, I am, too. About him making the trip alone, about his arriving in Newark around midnight alone, and, in all honesty? About my having to spend the next seven days alone.

Ok, that's not completely true. I won't be all alone. Casey and the dogs will be there. But I'll be down a kid, and since Stu's death I have a thing about keeping my sons close.

"Ugh, Usher," I reply as he successfully nudges his way from KIIS FM to Hits 1. "Not listening to Mr. Sex Songs, dude."

I figure he'll switch stations, but no. Instead he pops the radio off with the tip of his sweet, freckled ski jump of a nose and flops back in the passenger seat.

"What do you think Usher's mother thinks of his stuff?" he asks.

I love how my boy's brain works. I'd never in a million years think to ask that question or any of the others he barrages me with on a daily basis. Things like, *If the Catholics control Heaven, do they let the Jews in? What kind of sports do you think guys who become Navy Seals played when they were kids?* And my least favorite, *What happens to me and Casey if you get cancer?*

"Seriously," he prods, "what do you think Usher's mother thinks?"

"I think she thinks, 'Thanks for the penthouse, honey, but don't let your grandmother catch you singing that crap.'" He laughs and then it hits me. My son is on his way to see *his* grandmother, a.k.a. my mother, and if she catches him listening to Usher or any of his ilk, she'll kill me.

"Cuy," I start, but he knows where I'm headed and stops me.

"I know, I know. No Usher at Grandma's. No *Family Guy*, either right?"

"Good God, no. We'll both be out of the will."

At that we both crack up and then, without so much as a "Jeez, I'm sick of sitting here," he hops out of the car. His camouflage backpack, filled with clothes he'll try to avoid wearing and a toothbrush he'll try to avoid using right up until the moment my mom questions his lack of laundry and abundant bad breath, bounces as he strides purposefully across the parking lot, into the train station and out onto the tracks.

"Dude, what are you doing?"

"Mom, please," he responds, grinning with mock impatience and stretching his arms wide to steady himself as he use one of the rails as a balance beam. "Can't you see I'm going for the gold?"

"And can't you see I'm going to tear up this ticket if you don't get on this platform now?"

He ignores me and I stand there pretending to be annoyed. I know in my heart he's not going to get hurt. For starters, no matter what "Julie" claims, there is no train, and there probably won't be one for another hour. But more importantly, lately I've been filled with the feeling that, at least for the time being, my sons have a pass, a sort of God-given "Get Out of Jail, Free" card. Of course, they certainly shouldn't tempt fate by playing on train tracks, but for now, while they continue to recover and heal and learn to navigate their new normal, I really believe they're getting a little extra protection from above.

Maybe I'm deluding myself. Maybe I just can't stand the thought of losing someone else that I love. Or maybe, just maybe, my faith is on the money.

"We should call 'Julie' again."

I didn't even see him approach but suddenly, there he is. Safe and sound and smiling on the platform beside me. There's still no sign of a train, but "Julie" insists we'll see one in less than twenty minutes.

Perfect, I think. Just enough time to review the rules. No talking to strangers. Be aware of your environment. And for Pete's sake, no Usher, Pitbull, *South Park*, *Tosh.O*, or *Family Guy* at Grandma's.

Yes, I believe with my whole heart that God's keeping a close eye on my kids. But trust me when I tell you that if my mom discovers him watching or listening to any of that stuff, not even a force field of divine proportions will be able to save him.

The D-word

"They look awesome, Sue," said my brother's friend Marc when I stepped out of the dressing room in a pair of Levi's Demi Curve, dark rinse straight leg jeans. I glanced in the mirror. They looked ok. I squatted down. No plumber's crack, and they didn't explode off my butt and blind the sales kid standing behind me. Both good signs. But still, I wasn't sure. They were a little young and I'm, you know, a little not.

"You have to get those," my brother Nick insisted, caressing a grey sweater he'd quickly decide would be better in navy, and then better in black, and then, ultimately, best if he just put it back on the table. "You *need* to get those. They're hot, they're sexy," he paused for effect and smiled. "They're a whole new Sue."

I laughed. Little brothers: can't live with them, and it's still illegal to kill them.

"Nick, you're not helping!" Marc teased. He walked toward me making a little swirling motion with his index finger which, under regular circumstances I'd assume to mean *Nick is nuts* but, since I was trying on clothes, I knew he meant *Spin around so we make sure you don't leave the store looking like Snooki*, so I did.

"He's right," Marc decreed. "You have to get them."

"Really, Sue," Nick added, "they're what all the new widows are wearing."

At that the three of us completely lost it, and the poor sales kid who could still see but who probably wished he'd gone deaf the moment we walked in, simply looked at me like, *He's kidding, right?* I felt so bad for him. He wanted to make the sale, but I could see the hesitation (not to mention, horror), all over his face. Should he really push a pair of hot but just-this-side-of-snug jeans on a widow when there's probably a perfectly good nun's habit available on eBay?

"Enough," Marc announced. "We'll take them."

We will?

"I don't need these," I protested. "And I'm not going to wear them."

"Yes you do, and you are," Marc replied, grabbing me by the shoulders and pushing me toward the dressing room. "They'll look great with your little leopard print heels, won't they Nick?"

"Oh. Sure. Leopard print," Nick replied. "Why didn't I think of that?"

"And besides," Marc added, "they're the perfect 'date' jean."

The dressing room door slammed behind me. Did he just use the D-word? I hadn't told anyone I'd been on a few dates. Could he tell? Was I giving off some sort of scent? If so, it could only be the aroma of Eau de Bad Idea.

If you've ever wondered how to make a man spill his drink or slice himself with a steak knife, just tell him you're a widow with two kids, one of whom has autism, and you live on a farm in the middle of nowhere. It works like a charm. It's also typically followed by the words "Check please!" In all seriousness, I'd been out with a few men, all of whom were very nice, but not one of whom was in any condition to see anybody but a therapist. Separated and in pain. Divorced and navigating a maze of romantic entanglements that rivaled a soap opera. I didn't have the bandwidth or the desire to deal with their baggage.

Let's face it, I hadn't yet dealt with my own.

I missed feeling like Superwoman. While Stu was sick, I got up every day with one purpose: to keep him alive and take care of the boys. My men needed me and that's all I needed to keep going.

But then he died, and the marathon I'd been running was done. I crossed the finish line a loser. I had never felt pain like that, and I couldn't get away from it fast enough. If I could have scratched myself out of my skin to escape it, I would have. Instead, I became the non-stop cleaning machine I've already described.

I knew I had to get a grip. I was running – away – on fumes and for some reason I thought going out and having some fun would make me feel better. So, I went out, when what I really needed to do was go in, inside myself, and face my fears straight on. I had to feel my loss and make peace with my grief. I had to hold my fears up to the light and see how scary they weren't. I had to dig deep and do the work if I wanted to feel like Superwoman again.

There would be no more going out, no dating, until I was whole.

I looked at myself in the dressing room mirror. I doubted the jeans were what all the new widows were wearing, and I didn't really need them, but I liked them, and I knew Superwoman would too.

Who Knew My Kid Could Read So Much into a Cookie?

"Do you want to talk about Dad?"

Casey shakes his head *no*, grabs a package of *Chips Ahoy!* from the pantry, and heads back to the very loud Madden game he's engrossed in against Cuyler. I hear something like, "*Give me one of those*," followed by something like, "*Stuff it, small man*," and then Cuyler appears in the kitchen where I'm standing holding a second package of the coveted snack.

"Thanks, mom," he says, taking it from me. I smile my *you're welcome*, and he reaches out and hugs me.

"Cuy, come on!" Casey hollers from the den. "You're holding up the game!"

"You know he's gonna cheat if you don't get in there," I whisper, hugging my not so small man tight. In the last few weeks, he's hit a growth spurt and is now not only taller than me, but his voice seems to come from the soles of his super huge feet.

Cuy laughs but doesn't let go of my neck. "You ok, mom?"

"I have this feeling," I reply, breaking his embrace, grabbing the cookies, peeling open the package and popping one in my mouth in one smooth move, "that you guys want to talk about Dad, but for some reason nobody's sayin' nothin'."

Cuyler just stands there in his TEAMWORK Is A Whole Lot of People Doing What I Say tee shirt, black basketball shorts, and enormous black and red sneakers, staring at me. Or, more accurately, my mouth. He's seen me eat an entire roast chicken by myself in one sitting, but junk food? Just once, when Stu first got sick. I came home late one night from the hospital, scared and tired, and inhaled a bag of Tostitos. And then I spent the next two days looking like a blonde blowfish.

The cookie's hit the spot though, and for a split second I consider having another. Giving into temptation I reach out and Cuy responds by clutching the package to his chest with one hand and catapulting himself across our huge butcher block table with the other.

"Dude, what are you doing?"

"What are *you* doing?" He replies, incredulously.

"What are both of you doing?" demands Casey, coming into the kitchen and glancing from me to his brother and back again.

"Mom had a cookie," Cuy offers.

"Yeah?" Casey replies, eyeing me. "Something's weird with you today."

"She was going for a second, but I stopped her."

"Two cookies?" It was Casey's turn to be incredulous.

Cuyler nodded and came around the table still holding the chocolate chips tight to his chest. "I think it has something to do with Dad. She sort of asked me if I wanted to talk about him."

"Me, too."

Both boys looked at me like I was some kind of incompetent. *Brats*, I thought. Since when does my wanting a snack make it ok for the kids to talk about me right in front of me? But then, since when do I snack?

"Excuse me," I start, annoyed at my out-of-the-blue junk food jones, my kids for calling me on it, and the fact that they're both looking down on me while I'm gearing up to reprimand them, "you do realize I'm standing here, right?"

Cuyler looks at his feet, but Casey lets me have it.

"And you realize you're the one who wants to talk about Dad, right? I'm going back to the game."

"It's almost football season!" I call as he lopes off, ducking under the doorjamb and slamming the door to the den behind him. "Giants season," I say, turning to Cuy. "I just thought maybe you guys were missing him, you know, more."

"It's always going to be some season, mom," Cuy says softly. "And he's dead. So, unless there's some kind of miracle, my guess is we're always gonna miss him." He pauses and flicks the freshness seal on the package. "You really want another?" he asks.

"Nope. Just wanted to know if you wanted to talk."

He smiles and shakes his head, and I run my hand through his wavy, chocolate brown hair. "Go. Get on with your game," I say.

"And you get on with your life," he replies.

Excuse me?

"Face it, mom," he continues, looking past me to the closed den door behind which Casey is hooting and hollering and clearly cheating his way to victory over his brother's coach-less team, "you only snack when you're sad."

"Listen, Sigmund—" I start, but he cuts me off.

"No, you listen. You only snack when you're sad. But the thing is, you're not sad. You're happy. Annoyingly, sickeningly, disgustingly to the point of driving me and Casey crazy, happy," he replies. "And you feel guilty about it. Like you're hurting Dad, or you don't deserve it or whatever. Well you're not, and you do. Capeeshe?"

I stand there, stunned. Since when did my younger son get to be so perceptive? So empathetic? So eloquent?

"You got that from a cookie?" I ask.

"No. 'South Park'," he snaps, looking at me like I'm totally trying his patience. "The 'Jersey Shore' episode. You know, the one the four of us watched the other night. The *four* of us, mom" he adds, hinting hard at the reason for my newfound happiness and pangs of guilt.

And then he turned and went into the den. Done with me and my weird snacking, and desperate, I'm sure, to save what was left of his season.

Bounce Boost

I hate it when my kids call me out on my crap. I'm always positive I can keep how I'm feeling to myself by putting on an Oscar-worthy performance in a play I call "This Is Not Bothering Me" right up to the moment one of my sons bursts my bubble by stating the obvious, and I'm reminded once again that I'll never be the next Meryl Streep.

In all seriousness though, I should have realized the boys would sense something was up. All I had to do was say, *Hey guys, can we talk? I'm bursting with happiness and I feel awful about it.* Both kids would have given me their "no guilt, get on with your life" lecture (but not a cookie), and that would have been that.

After all, they got the "no guilt" stuff from me. And I got it from Ellen.

"Guilt," she said, "is like sitting in a rocking chair. It'll give you something to do, but it's not going to get you anywhere. It's a completely wasted emotion."

For a long while after Stu's death, I felt guilty for not having insisted he get a second opinion early on in his illness. But every time I brought it up, he told me I was overreacting, he didn't need another opinion. "I trust these guys," he'd say. Well, "these guys" misdiagnosed him and we lost three months of fighting the cancer he was riddled with while "these guys" put stent after stent in his bile duct, never seeing the tumor sitting there in plain sight.

Even now, nine years later, if I think too much about that time, I can still feel guilty for not fighting harder. So, I don't let myself think about it anymore. Guilt robs us of today, its weight leaves us too exhausted to enjoy tomorrow, and it doesn't change anything.

And as for feeling guilty for going on with my life and for having a life to go on with, yes, I felt badly about it at first but I don't anymore and here's why: I'm the mom. It is, was, and always will be my responsibility to set the example for my sons and to remind them that, at the end of the day, our one and only job is to live and enjoy our one and only life.

Will we see today through? Wake up tomorrow morning? Who knows? So, get out there and get on with it. And no guilt.

The Winemaker

In the summertime, the main street in our town is closed on the first Friday night of the month. The shops stay open late, sometimes a band plays, there's activities for kids to do, and families pushing strollers and walking dogs come out in droves. It was on one of those First Fridays that I saw him. My friend Jenn and I were going in and out of the shops that were offering wine tastings, sipping a Cabernet here and a Chardonnay there, when we stepped out into the street and he was standing in the middle of it surrounded by women. I couldn't take my eyes off him; he looked like a movie star.

"Who is *that?*" I asked.

"That's the Winemaker," she replied.

We were about twenty feet away, watching him hold court, when he started dancing with one of his admirers. I can't recall if there was any music playing, but I very clearly remember watching him dip her and then kiss her and thinking, Wow, I wish he'd kiss me like that.

I've since learned to be more careful about what I wish for.

****

In no time, we were a couple. And Cuyler was right; I was sickeningly happy. Why wouldn't I be? The Winemaker took me everywhere. To parties and restaurant openings and wine tastings, to England to meet his family, and to St. Michael's to relax over spring break. We were the "it" couple. The recently widowed, local author and the popular winemaker; big fish in the small but beautiful pond known as Fauquier County, Virginia.

Our whirlwind romance was like something out of a fairy tale which, in hindsight, should have been my first clue that all was not what it appeared to be.

The Winemaker swooped in like a knight in shining armor, as if he knew simply by looking at me that I was overwhelmed, lonely, vulnerable, and still grieving, and wanted to save me. In and of itself, this is lovely, but something didn't sit right with me. One moment we're dating, the next we're together almost 24 hours a day, seven days a week. It was so much, so fast. I went ages without seeing my friends, days without seeing my sons, and when I was home, the Winemaker was there, too.

My gut, intuition, radar, Spidey Sense, whatever you want to call it, nagged at me. *He's moving too fast, Susan,* it said. *He rarely includes your sons, Susan*, it nudged. *Where are your boundaries, woman?* it hollered. But I didn't want to hear it. I told myself my radar was rusty, that I was still "recovering" and thus overthinking things. I wanted to enjoy the gifts and trips and flowers and the feeling of being alive. I wanted to believe the attention this handsome man showered me with was because he loved me. I wanted to see what I wanted to see, feel how I wanted to feel, and believe what I wanted to believe: that the Winemaker was wonderful.

Only he wasn't.

Eight months into our relationship he proposed, and two thoughts sprang into my head simultaneously: *It's too soon.* and *Hesitate, and he's gone.*

I didn't want to lose him. I loved him. I said yes.

Shortly thereafter, the Winemaker went out of town for six weeks and I spent that time in a state of high anxiety, refereeing an exhausting battle between my what I was telling myself and what my gut was telling me, fighting back-to-back sinus infections, and suffering a serious bout of depression; all tell-tale signs I was headed in a direction I didn't want to go. And then, just a few weeks before

Cuy and I were supposed to move into his house, leaving the farm after eight years, my intuition and the Universe teamed up for one last attempt to get my attention.

I was driving Cuy to a flag-football game when I became distracted by a group of kids from the high school standing in front of a medical building holding big, handwritten signs that said Car Wash! and Support the Booster Club! The fact that they were right outside Blueridge Orthopedics promoting a fundraiser that was at the high school confused me for some reason and as we passed I glanced at them twice, the second time at the same time the light turned red, the car ahead of us came to a dead stop, and we did not.

Thankfully, no one was hurt and the damage to the car I hit was minimal, but my pretty little Buick Enclave would be out of commission for weeks. As I stood there, talking with the police officer taking the report, it occurred to me that this was a sign from above not just telling me to stop but making me stop.

If only I'd listened.

We were married on Father's Day and left for our honeymoon a few days later. About two weeks after we returned, we were sitting around the table one night after dinner, talking and drinking wine. A lot of wine. Too much wine. I know that now, but then it was the norm. The Winemaker had had a setback that day at work. A visual one of his marketing people created and that The Washington Post planned to use in an article on the Virginia wine industry had a mistake in it. Sadly, it was the Post and not one of the Winemaker's people who caught it and thus the paper would not be running it with the story. He was angry about it and honestly, I couldn't blame him.

Because of my past experience in marketing, I knew how valuable such exposure was. I also knew that if I'd made a similar mistake or if someone in my department had done so and I hadn't caught it, there'd be hell to pay. I could lose my job for blowing such an opportunity and, even if I didn't, I'd feel terrible about it.

So, I said something to the effect of, I'm sorry about the Post thing, sweetheart. Such a missed opportunity.

He slammed his glass on the table and shook his head like he was dealing with a child. "I don't make those decisions," he said, glaring at me.

My stomach clenched. "Of course, you didn't make the decision," I replied, "but it was such a great opportunity. You must feel badly about it."

He leaned in toward me, his face inches away from mine. "I just told you," he said, "I don't make those decisions."

I wish I could tell you that it was the wine that made me do what I did next, but I can't because it wasn't. Since Cuyler and I moved in with him a month before the wedding, and since the day of, I'd begun to see the things my intuition tried to warn me about. Angry rages. Bullying. Paranoia. Split second mood swings. The man who wined and dined and took me everywhere under the sun, the man I sat talking and laughing with late into the evenings, the man who introduced me to family and friends and associates like I was the most wonderful, beautiful, lovely creature he'd ever encountered, was gone. Gone. Like he never existed. Worse still, I was no longer wonderful, beautiful, and lovely. I was just another one of the "morons" he had to deal with every day. Just another of his employees he insisted couldn't communicate properly, follow orders, stole from him, and who were trying to destroy his business.

(For the record, I never saw a shred of evidence of any of that. What I saw were people who came to work every day proud to pour his wines and share the intricacies of each with every customer who walked into his tasting room. What I saw were people who didn't quit despite the frequency with which he'd blow into the winery, see their lunches someplace he'd suddenly decide they didn't belong, stick out one of his long, powerful arms and in one angry swoop, sweep them onto the floor, splattering sandwiches, salads, containers of mac and cheese, and open cans of soda everywhere. What I saw were people who tolerated having a tape gun rocket over their heads and stick to the wall when he was in a rage. What I saw were people who came in on their day off, spouses, significant others, and out of town guests in tow, because they were so proud to be part of his team. What I saw were people who used to work there but who'd moved to North Carolina, South Carolina, Florida, wherever, come in to work for him every time they returned to Virginia to visit. He could be so cruel to them, and yet they loved him.)

I knew I should shut up. The conversation was going south, and I was scared. After a year of ignoring my gut, it hurt so much to realize that it had been right all along. But still, I wanted proof, so I pushed.

"Honey," I said, "I'm sorry. I'm not making myself clear. I know you didn't make the decision, but if something like this had happened when I worked in New York–"

His fist slamming my mouth finished my sentence.

"No one," he hissed, leaning into my face, "gives a shit how you did things in New York."

He ripped open the front door and drove off while I sat there with my lips swelling and bleeding, my heart breaking, and my gut saying, well, now we know why he was in such a rush to get married.

He couldn't keep his act up much longer. He couldn't keep pretending to be someone he isn't.

I know now that I married a malignant narcissist. I know now that the swirl of gifts, trips, flowers, and fancy dinners is called love-bombing and that the narcissist employs it to maintain a constant supply of adoration.

So why hit me and cut off the supply?

Because a narcissist doesn't want to be a member of any club that will have him and, once you're married to a narcissist, you're in that club. The moment I said, "I do," I was done. Immediately, I was devalued and doomed to be treated the way narcissists treat everyone – with disdain, rage, and bullying, with emotional, psychological, and often physical abuse.

Sometimes I feel badly for the Winemaker. He's sentenced to a lifetime of repeating this cycle. And then I think back to the day he tried to kill me and Cuyler, and quickly come to my senses.

Cuy and I left not long after that incident and I have never ignored my gut again.

Part Three

THE END AND THE BEGINNING

"You don't need to see the whole staircase, just take the first step."

Martin Luther King Jr.

The New C-word

I haven't taken two steps onto the track when my phone lights up with my boss's name. It's a Monday at 9 a.m. and I should be at my desk. I'm not because I knew his call was coming and I wanted to be outside when it did.

Getting laid off in the sunshine I can handle.

Getting laid off in the middle of doing the job that I love I cannot.

I answer with a laugh and say something along the lines of "Bruce! What a surprise to hear from you so bright an early!"

He gives me a half laugh and starts talking. He sounds awful. I almost can't hear what he's telling me because I feel so bad that he has to make these phone calls. I'm furloughed for a few weeks. Hopefully ad pages will pick up and we can put out a May issue. Or skip May and go straight to June. I say sure, that sounds great. He tells me everything he and the partners are doing to keep the company afloat. I say thank you. He says I'm sorry. We hang up.

We are in the midst of the Coronavirus.

****

I spend a lot of time at the track, walking three miles one day, five the next. While I walk, I work on this book, grateful for the trip back in time it's taking me on. Grateful to escape this crisis even if it's to revisit those in the past. Grateful to be able to remind myself that the boys and I have weathered other storms and we will weather this one, too.

When Mother Nature says, "Now!"

The day Cuyler and I fled the Winemaker was not the day we were supposed to flee the Winemaker. We were supposed to go the day our apartment was ready. But you know what they say: make plans and God laughs, this time along with Mother Nature.

I kept an eye on the Winemaker's car, which was parked in front of the winery, while Cuy stuffed practically everything he owns into the BMW. His video game console, video games, rugby gear, laptop, photos, favorite pillow, clothing, contact lenses, school stuff; if it fit in a box or a bag, he packed it and somehow squeezed all of it into our two-door convertible. Then he watched the Winemaker's car while I grabbed my laptop, some clothes, and my makeup. Next to nothing compared to his haul.

It hadn't been thirty-minutes since I snapped off the Weather Channel, said, "Cuy, we're getting a snowstorm. Let's get out of here," before we were in the car, flakes beginning to fall, racing to the safety of Jenn's house.

It's an understatement to say that both Cuy and I were more than a little concerned at the prospect of being snowed in with the Winemaker. There would be no making a fire and relaxing by the fireplace, playing games, or reading books during the break Mother Nature was about to give us. There would be no looking out the window, savoring the different shaped flakes and the beauty of the grapevines covered in snow. There would only be rage. Rage from the moment he awakened, saw the snow, and went off on one of his frightening diatribes during which he'd stomp from the bedroom to the kitchen and back again, in various stages of getting dressed, alternately barking about the laziness of his employees, my talent for screwing up the filter in his fish tank (*No matter how many times I show you! No matter how many times!*), railing about the inability of Americans to drive in snow, their shitty work ethic, and how he has to do everything himself. Then he'd blow out the door, do ninety in five feet of snow down to the winery, do I don't know what for three minutes, then race back to the house, into the kitchen, and tear toward Cuyler's room where he'd find me, shaking but blocking the door, and derailing his plans to mercilessly bully and belittle my son simply because there was no one else around to torture.

This is how our snow day would go, all day, and for every day we were snowed in. Sadly, it didn't have to be snowing for this to happen, but the snow meant we were stuck in the house, sentenced to the Winemaker's rollercoastering rage.

"We're not going back this time, right?" Cuy asked, buckling his seatbelt as we took off down the driveway.

I shook my head no.

"We've gone back twice. Please don't make us go back," he pleaded.

"We're not going back. Ever. We're going to Jenn's and then we're moving into the apartment Marina found."

He sighed and relaxed a little into the passenger seat. A moment passed.

"Jenn knows we're on our way, right?"

Shit.

"Can you dig out my phone?" I responded.

"Nice, mom," he replied, rolling his eyes and rooting around in my bag. "We're practically on her doorstep and now you're calling her? We're going to wind up back there! What if she's not home? You said– "

"Phone please."

Jenn answered on the second ring.

"You know how you said we could stay with you if we needed to leave before the apartment's ready?"

"Hello to you too and of course I do!" she replied. "I absolutely told you to come. You better come! When are you coming?"

"Now."

"Now?"

"Yeah, sorry," I paused. "We should be there in ten. I'll explain when we arrive ok?"

"More than ok, sweet thing. I can't wait. It'll be a snowstorm sleepover!"

I clicked off and glanced at my son. "Better?" I asked, handing him my phone.

He shrugged. "You think he'll wreck all the stuff we couldn't take? Come looking for us?"

I shook my head, no.

"That would mean he cares, Cuy, and he doesn't. He didn't care about us when we lived there, and he's not going to care that we're gone."

We drove in silence for a bit, Cuy tapping on his phone while I mentally reviewed the list of people I needed to call when we arrived at Jenn's: my attorney, my bother in law Doug, and my friend Michele, the domestic abuse specialist at the Sherriff's department.

But the person I needed to call first was my mom. She was the one I'd called just a few weeks earlier, when the Winemaker, Cuyler, and I were on our way home from her house the day after Christmas.

We were on the highway somewhere in Delaware, doing the Winemaker's preferred speed of almost 100 miles per hour. He was hungry and insistent we find someplace cool to have lunch. I had no idea where "someplace cool" was and made the mistake – big mistake – of saying so.

"Use your phone!" he screamed. "How come you don't know how to use your phone?! I can't drive and search at the same time!"

I immediately started to shake. He's screaming, driving at the speed of sound, and Cuy is in the back seat.

"Sweetheart," I said, "I'd really like to get home. Can't we just stop at a Subway?"

"You want to stop? Just stop? Sure. We'll just stop."

He slammed on the brakes. The car pitched forward. From the corner of one eye, I saw Cuyler's head slam into the back of the driver's seat. From the other, I saw the dashboard coming fast for my face. I didn't connect, but only because the Winemaker punched me in the chest with such force it stopped me mid-flight.

Then he sped off the highway, into a strip mall, and gunned it for a glass storefront. I screamed for him to stop, so he obliged, hitting the brakes just seconds before we hit the glass. In a nanosecond, he exploded from the car, raced to the passenger seat behind me, grabbed his laptop, and ran away. Not a moment later, Cuyler and his brand-new driver's license were at the wheel.

"We're not waiting for that asshole and we're not looking for him. We're leaving," he said.

And so, we drove home, stopping only so Cuy could get something to eat and I could call my mom.

"Gotta call grandma," I said, turning into Jenn's driveway at the top of a huge hill. It was the perfect place to be snowed in. We wouldn't be able to get down the mountain, and no one would be able to get up. Not that I expected anyone to try; I meant what I said to Cuyler. But it's always nice to have a little insurance. And a dear friend to run to when Mother Nature says, "now!"

PTED
(Post Traumatic Ex-husband Disorder)

Nights become an endless, panicked search for my sons through a dark and terrifying landscape that changes with every corner I turn. One minute, I'm hiding in a doorway as buildings thunder to the ground around me. The next, I'm thrashing in the tall grasses of an enormous field, entire sections of which are burning. Panic has me by the throat. I swallow hard and with every ounce of strength I can muster, scream my sons' names.

Nothing. No reply. My kids are out there, somewhere, lost, scared, maybe hurt or worse. How could I have let this happen? Nausea rises in my throat.

Suddenly, Casey is beside me. My legs buckle with relief as I reach for him.

"There's no time, mom," he says. "We've got to go!"

He grabs my hand and starts to run. Only I can't. I'm barely able to walk, my legs are so heavy. He lets go of me and I struggle, arms outstretched, watching helplessly as my first born gets further and further away from me, disappearing into the tall grass.

I've lost him, I think, *I've lost them.* I collapse on my hands and knees, sobbing and rocking back and forth, faster and faster in the grass. *Please God, save my sons*, I cry. *Get them home. I have to get them home!*

"Mom!"

I open my eyes and Cuy's staring down at me, shaking me hard by the shoulders. There are tears in his eyes. He's dressed for school and his backpack is on my bedroom floor.

"This is the third time in two weeks!" he yells. "You're scaring the shit out of me!"

I nod and sit up. My heart is pounding in my chest. My face is soaked with tears. I look around my baby blue bedroom with such relief I could cry. Again. "That was a bad one," I say.

"You're telling me?" He grabs his backpack and turns on his heel as last night's dinner conversation slowly comes back to me. He's going in early to train. After school he has rugby practice so he's taking the car. He won't be home until around nine. *Everyone is safe*, I think. *Oh, thank God, they're safe.* I close my eyes briefly; the blackness threatens to suck me back in and a sob escapes my throat. *Stop it*, I think. *Snap out of it! It was just a dream.*

I can hear Cuy in the kitchen getting the car keys and grabbing a Gatorade from the fridge. When he leaves, I'll hear the sliding glass door slam shut. If he goes without saying good-bye it will be the first time that's ever happened and that can't happen. I run into the hall to catch him and stop short; he's walking toward me.

"Cuy," I start. "I'm sorry."

"Mom stop," he says. "There's no need for you to be sorry. We're home. We're safe." He drops his million-pound backpack to the carpet and hugs me. "You did it. You got us out of there. He can't terrorize me for sport anymore, mom. He can't throw Casey down the stairs ever again. And most importantly, he can't hit you and bully you and make you think you're the crazy one anymore."

Now I really want to cry. Instead, I hug him tighter and say, "C'mon. You'll be late."

I walk with him through the living room, out the sliding glass doors and onto our concrete patio.

"Give kiss, Cuyler," I say, like I've said every day since he went to daycare, and he responds the same way he's responded every day since the day he went to daycare, by giving me the top of his head to kiss.

"Nice," I tease, and then call after him. "What does it take for a mom to get a little 'off to school' smooch around here?"

I stand there in my sweats and sleep tee and watch him walk away. The playground our patio looks out on is empty but there are people – our neighbors, actually – out, walking their dogs and cleaning up after them. We know some of them already, so I wave and yell good morning. I'm certain I look like hell; my leftover mascara must be all over my face from crying but I stand there, breathing in the new day and thanking God that I can enjoy it from this small, sweet patio and the lovely, safe apartment to which it's attached.

I'm about to go in and make coffee when I see Cuy jogging back to me.

"I'll tell you," he says, stopping just short of knocking me down.

"Tell me what? That you're planning on tackling me?"

"No. Listen," he says, jogging in place like he does when he knows he's about to be late. "I'll tell you what it takes to get an off to school smooch."

"Ok," I smile.

"You need to call Laurie or Ellen and tell them what's going on."

"Ah ha!" I cry. "So, you're playing the therapist card?"

"Nope! I'm playing the therapists card," he replies, emphasizing the "s" in therapists so it sounds like therapistists. "I know there's two and I don't care which one you call as long as you call."

"And if I do, you'll stop giving me the top of your head to kiss?"

"Yes!" he cries, jogging backwards up the sloping hill toward the parking lot.

"Can we start now?" I yell.

"Have you called yet?" He shouts back.

"No, but I will, I will!" I yell, jumping up and down and making him laugh.

"Nyet!" he cries.

And with one fast, fell swoop, he's in the car, giving me a wave, and gone.

Bounce Boost

I want that off-to-school smooch and making the nightmares go away would be great, so I call Ellen and Laurie as soon as the coffee is brewing. I get both their voicemails, hesitate, and hang up.

Is it possible I don't really want a kiss good-bye from my kid? Is it possible I don't mind being sucked into the seventh circle of hell every few nights?

No, it's not. But the reality is that I'm ashamed of myself for being swept off my feet by a phony, for ignoring my intuition, and for putting the boys in harm's way. I'm ashamed for not leaving the first time he hit me, not leaving the night he threw Casey down a flight of stairs, not leaving as his bullying of Cuyler escalated, and not leaving immediately after he nearly killed us all in the car.

But the thing I'm most ashamed of is the grief and heartache bubbling beneath my skin.

****

It's been several years since that morning and, when I think back on it, two things come to mind.

First, when it comes to shame, don't give in to that shit.

Author and shame researcher, Brene Brown, has said that, "Shame cannot survive being spoken and it cannot survive empathy." So, the thing to do is to tell someone you trust, someone who'll understand and empathize, about the thing or things you feel ashamed of. I promise you, when you and your trusted someone hold that "thing" up to the light, you're going to laugh. And cry. And laugh some more.

Second, when we lose someone we love, we grieve. It's that simple.

I'd fallen in love with a man who didn't exist, with whom every memory I made during our time together was, at its core, fake, a fairy tale, a daydream. I grieved because I had loved him. I felt as if not just the rug, but the entire earth had been pulled out from beneath me.

Over time, just as I did when Stu died, I made peace with my grief. I sat with it, let it become part of me, and decided I'd use it to do something good in my little corner of the Universe. I had no idea what that would be, but, as it turned out, the Universe had a few thoughts on the matter.

P.S. Ultimately, I shared all my shame and grief and pain with Ellen. It took a while for the nightmares to stop, but I got that off-to-school smooch the next day.

And Then She Came Along

I'm sitting at my desk in our sweet little lemon-heavy apartment one morning when I get an email from a friend. Since she's an advertising salesperson for our local paper, and since the paper is always so generous about promoting my work, I figure her note must have something to do with that. So, I open it.

"Hi Susan," it says. "We're launching a brand-new women's magazine and we'd like you to be the editor. If you're interested, we'd love to get together and share our ideas and vision with you. Let me know!"

If I'm interested? Being the editor of a magazine is something I've dreamed of doing for years. Seriously. Since I was eighteen.

After high school, I commuted from New Jersey to New York to attend Marymount Manhattan College. Neither of my parents were too thrilled I was in the city and both made me promise I'd never set foot in the subway so, once I got to the Port of Authority at Eighth Avenue and 42nd Street, I had to take two more buses to get to school. One across 42nd Street to Third Avenue, and the other up Third Avenue to 71st Street. When my classes were over for the day, I reversed the trip, taking the bus down Lexington Avenue to 42nd Street where I'd either catch the crosstown bus or walk the rest of the way to the Port of Authority.

I loved my commute utterly and completely. Did it almost every day for four years and the best part was the trip up Third Avenue. Every morning I took a seat in the middle of the bus and watched out the window until my favorite building came into view. Near the top of it, the offices had enormous floor-to-ceiling windows of varying tints. Some were smoky, others were black, and still others were completely clear. My favorite, the corner office, had clear glass windows and I liked to imagine that in that huge space, with the sunlight pouring in, someone was putting together a magazine. Every time I passed it, I imagined an editor sitting at her spacious desk, reviewing layouts, deciding on the cover, planning the next issue. For some strange reason, that glass office said "magazine" to me from the moment I laid eyes on it my freshman year. And oh yes, if there *was* a magazine being published in there, I wanted to work there.

Except that I didn't want to starve. My parents were worried I'd pursue a writing career and would starve to death waiting for my first paying assignment that might never come because, well, I might not be that talented. I agreed that food was important and thus, font of confidence that I was, made a beeline into marketing before the ink was dry on my diploma.

Being a marketing director is one of those jobs that people refer to as a "big" job. It has a certain amount of prestige and is the kind of position people aspire to. I, on the other hand, still aspired to be – you guessed it – the editor. Part of that is because I had such a great editor. She was a smart, classy, generous lady who on more than a few occasions invited me to talk with her about my writing. That was a treat. I'd go into her office and breathe in the beautifully photographed layouts that covered the walls, steal a peek at the manuscripts open on her desk, and occasionally catch snippets of conversation between her and the food editor or, even better, the beauty editor.

Getting such one-on-one time with the editor-in-chief is not usually the norm. One reason is because he or she is the EDITOR-IN-CHIEF. Another is because in magazine publishing, editorial is considered Church, and the business side, of which marketing is a part, is considered State. As such there isn't a lot of hanging out and getting chummy, nor do you typically find editorial folks making the jump to the business (sales and marketing) side or someone on the marketing side making the switch to the editorial side.

Still though, I dreamt about it.

Of course, I'd forgotten about that dream right up until the moment I opened that email, reread it five times, thinking, *This is my dream job. I would love to do this job. I want this job!* And then, almost as immediately, *I can't do this job. I don't have the experience to do this job. I'll fail. Or worse, I'll get fired!*

Quickly, I forwarded the email to my friend Trish with a note that said, "Look at this – it's my dream job!! Too bad I don't have a clue how to do it!"

Not ten seconds after I hit send, my cell rang. Now cell phones do lots of things – they ding, they beep, they vibrate with all kinds of notifications – but they hardly ever ring. And when they do, or at least when mine does, it's usually one of the boys asking for money or telling me the car has a flat. But alas, it's Trish so I answer.

"You didn't respond, did you?" she practically shouted. "Tell me you didn't respond!"

"No," I said, "I'm still looking at it."

"Thank God!" she said, as if she caught me mere seconds before pulling the plug on the wrong patient. "Now here's what you're going to say."

Excuse me?

"Are you in the email?"

"Yes," I replied, "I'm in the email."

"Good. Type this up. Ready?'

"Sure," I said, completely unsure.

"Thank you for thinking of me," pause, "I'm so honored. I accept!"

Was she crazy?

"Trish, I can't send that. I don't know how to be a magazine editor!"

And then, with all the patience – which I sense is growing thin, if only because she thought I already responded and was petrified the "recall" function in my email wouldn't work – she can muster, she said, "Susan, think back to your marketing days. Do you not remember creating eight, ten, sixteen-page advertorials? Those are mini magazines! You could do this job with your eyes closed. Say yes."

"I can't, Trish."

"You can. Just say yes and figure it out later."

I took a deep breath and sent the following reply:

"I'd love to. Thank you! When should we get together?"

****

You know it went well because if it didn't, I wouldn't be telling you about it, right? The magazine, called SHE!, was a huge hit. Advertisers loved it. Readers loved it. The debut issue wasn't out a week before people began sending in checks for subscriptions which was crazy because we weren't offering subscriptions.

Oh yes, we immediately began offering subscriptions.

Not long after that, our local supermarket chain called and spoke with our distribution team. I wasn't privy to the call, but I've been told the conversation went something along these lines:

Local Supermarket Chain (LSC): Are you people responsible for this SHE! magazine our customers keep asking for?

SHE! Distribution Team (SDT): Your customers keep asking for SHE!?

LSC: Constantly. They're driving our managers nuts.

SDT: Awesome! I mean, it's not awesome they're driving your people nuts but, awesome!

LSC: Uh huh. Can you just help us get it in stock?

Of course we could, and did, immediately, yesterday almost.

If you're thinking, wow, Susan, you turned out to be a born editor, allow me to set the record straight. What I am is a born girlfriend collector – and all my girlfriends just happen to be incredibly talented.

Once I survived my panic attack over accepting a job under the "Say yes and figure it out later" school of thought, I opened my laptop and, don't laugh, my rolodex, and made a list of all the women I wanted to work with. I didn't have a budget to pay them, but I had free reign to promote them and their individual businesses on the contributors' page, at the bottom of the features they wrote, and across social media.

Not one of them said "no thanks," and in a few short emails team SHE! was in place.

Life couldn't get any better.

Or could it?

At a planning meeting for the first issue, I was introduced to my new art director, Meredith Hancock. Mer's very pretty, but beyond that and far more importantly, she's one of those people who oozes quiet confidence. Oh what I wouldn't do to ooze quiet confidence, to be the kind of person who, from their posture to the pace of their speech, radiates a deep knowledge of and comfort with what they bring to the party. I would love to be like that, to be a little sophisticated, maybe even mysterious.

Instead, I'm one of those people who bursts with enthusiasm for whatever I'm working on. This makes me anything but sophisticated and the only mystery is why none of my co-workers have ever tried to kill me. When I'm excited, the surplus of energy that fills my body like air racing into a balloon makes me talk too loud, too fast, and be far too happy. I was afraid Meredith was going to hate me. During the meeting I did my best to curb my enthusiasm, but it got the better of me. Before I knew it, I was in mega-happy mode, talking too fast, slipping into my New Jersey regionalism, and making people laugh.

"Way to make a good first impression, Suz," I thought, silently kicking myself for my ridiculous exuberance, when Meredith appeared at my side.

"They told me I'd love you," she said, "and I do. This is going to be great!"

It was great.

Every issue of SHE! was more beautiful than the one before, and I can't claim any credit for that. Meredith's design skills are killer, and Sandra Packwood, who oversaw fashion and beauty for the magazine, has a sense of style that's straight off 7th Avenue.

"Yes, we're pairing the leopard print jacket with the Sketchers," she once said to me. "Stop worrying! It works!"

I had three favorite days per issue. The first was fashion shoot day.

We shot all over Old Town Warrenton, on Main Street, in restaurants, and in event venues. While the photographer did her thing, I snapped photos and posted to social media. One time we shot at the hockey rink near the high school and my post, a cheerful "Shooting at the hockey rink today!" nearly gave our school Superintendent a heart attack.

My second favorite day was the day the photos came in from the photographer. Sandra and I would sit in my little lemony kitchen, drinking wine and gushing over every image. We'd select the photos for the fashion feature and the one for the cover. I'll never forget the night we selected Jenn's photo. The image came up and Sandra and I shouted "Cover!" and "Not telling her!" at the same time.

My third favorite day was the day the issue came out. People would stream into the newspaper office for copies. The sales staff would run off to deliver issues to advertisers. And the models featured in the issue – moms, grand moms, students, business professionals in all different sizes, shapes, and colors – would rush in for copies to share with their family and friends.

Meredith was right. It was great.

I loved that job, the people I got to work with, the friendships I made and still have today (so you can imagine how full my ancient rolodex is), and all that I learned, especially about myself.

My goal with SHE! was to have every issue feel like a visit with your best girlfriend. One of those visits that begins over coffee and ends over wine. One of those visits where you talk for hours, catching up, comparing notes, sometimes commiserating, about work, kids, spouses, houses, travel plans, aging parents, books, and how much you wish you had time to visit more frequently. I'm unsure I achieved that goal in its entirety, but I think I came close.

Over the eighteen months I edited SHE! I was also put in charge of two other quarterlies, one monthly, and all the special sections that appeared in the newspaper. I went from knowing nothing (although Trish will tell you otherwise), to absolute, if not quiet, confidence in my abilities.

I was in mega-happy mode the entire time.

Almost.

Ad pages started to slip across the board. There were layoffs. Ultimately it was decided that the newspaper had to focus first and foremost on being a newspaper. Many of the magazines, including SHE!, were shelved. It was sad, but then nothing good, or bad, lasts forever. And if I hadn't screwed up the courage to go for it, despite the very really possibility I could have failed, I would have missed all the good SHE! gave me.

There's a lot to be said about saying yes and figuring it out later, but I'll keep it to these two simple truths. One, if you say yes and you fail, so what? Failure isn't fatal but not trying something you want so badly you can taste it can leave you asking, "What if?" for the rest of your life. And two, if you say yes and you succeed, you've shown yourself that you just might be able to do anything, and that can leave you ready, willing, and eager to ask, "What's next?" for the rest of your life.

P.S. When the Universe brings you an opportunity that shoots lightning bolts of excitement through your body, that sets you ablaze with anticipation, that makes you salivate with the desire to say yes, you have to say yes. Why? Because here's the bottom line when it comes to the Universe: it doesn't put an opportunity in our path if it *isn't* for us to say yes to. So have faith in yourself and in the Universe. Say yes and figure it out later. I promise you, one way or another, you will.

Oh Please. "You Look So Healthy!" is Totally Code for "Girlfriend, You're Getting Fat!"

I'm speed walking along a wooded trail, dripping sweat, killing time while Cuyler wraps up rugby practice, and all I can hear are bees zipping past my head, and the sound of my way too tight, way too long yoga pants dragging in the dirt. They're too tight because when I bought them, I weighed far too little. They're too long because I meant to hem them, but I hate sewing almost as much as I hate speed walking in the heat, being stalked by bees, and not weighing far too little.

Now I realize that when a woman reaches a certain age, she has to make a decision: her figure or her face. Being of a certain age for a certain number of years now, I chose my figure, and figured a paper bag could handle my face. I even planned to wear one on my wedding day, but it clashed with my Sue Wong dress. Suffice it to say, I still wish I'd upgraded to the "Kate Hudson Photo-shopped Over Your Face" package as soon as I saw the proofs.

Of course if I were getting married tomorrow, I wouldn't be too worried about my face. Not because I'm suddenly so gorgeous, but because my signature, this-close-to-starving-to-death look is long gone. These days, when I run into people I haven't seen in a while, they say well-meanings things like, "You look so much better!" and "We were all worried about you!" and my personal favorite, "You look so healthy!"

Oh please. "You look so healthy" is totally code for "Girlfriend, you're getting fat."

And I am. Just ask my way too long, way too tight yoga pants (the bottoms of which are now sporting a rather lovely fringe of mud and leaves), and every other item of clothing in my closet. Correction: every other item of clothing that *used* to be in my closet but is now at my favorite consignment store. Absolutely nothing fits, at least nothing in my preferred size of "celery stalk" or, as Jenn once said, "stick insect."

If I may digress for just a moment, I took Jenn's comment as a compliment. Phasmids (aka, stick insects) are reed thin with long legs and they don't need a man to have kids. How in any way, shape, or form could that not be a compliment?

But the worst part of no longer being an honorary member of the Phasmid family is that I didn't choose to defect. I didn't wake up one morning and think, "Hmmm. Maybe it's not normal for women of a certain age to be able to share clothes with their nine-year-old nieces." No, I woke up one morning and could hardly get out of bed. I didn't know it at the time, but the searing pain running down the backs of both my legs, and the feeling like someone had beaten my hips with a two-by-four, was osteoarthritis. I also didn't know it was going to take seventeen vials of blood, one MRI, physical therapy, a daily dose of a kick-ass anti-inflammatory, and six months of barely being able to climb into my car let alone "grapevine" and "kick ball change" in my Jazzercise class before I'd feel like, if not look like, myself again.

But it did.

Cuy slides into the car, sucking down a Gatorade and reeking of sweat. I don't smell much better, but why miss a chance to tease him? I pinch my nose.

"Nice," he responds. "I saw you walking."

"I'm trying," I reply, patting the roll around my belly where my oblique muscles used to be.

"Oh yes," he quips, rolling his eyes. "As if I could possibly forget your ridiculous quest to wear the stuff you bought at Baby Gap."

"The booties still fit," I kid.

"You know what mom," he says in a tone that tells me we're thirty seconds from the end of this conversation, "you're not fat. You look fine. And if your clothes don't fit, throw them out and get new ones. That's what I'd do. And I'd start with those pants."

"I know, they're too tight."

"They're not too tight!" he snaps, exasperated. "Look at them. They're ripped to shreds. I play rugby and my gear's not that gross."

"So you're suggesting I look at this as an opportunity to go shopping."

"Yeah. Hit Justice or something," he smirks, toasting me with his second Gatorade. "That's where all the big girls go."

I pull onto the highway considering his idea. On the one hand, I could resume my killer workout/eat like a rabbit routine and count the days until the arthritis rears its ugly head and leaves me hobbled (or until the moment I have to have my picture taken and don't have the option of having my face replaced by Kate Hudson's).

Or I could buy some stuff that fits and see how I feel.

"Ok Cuyler," I say. "You're on."

"Proud of you, mom," he replies, turning on the radio, the universal signal for quality-time-with-your-teen-has-come-to-a-close. "Now we can stop all this discussion about your weight, and just be happy you finally look healthy."

Oh dear God, I'm getting fat.

My Apartment is Lemonade

When Cuy and I moved into the apartment I developed a real thing for lemons which I'm certain is because life just kept throwing them at me.

We weren't in the place a week when I parted ways with my longtime literary agent.

Losing her sent me into a tailspin. Before she came along, I was just another one of the millions of moms with blogs. But then she stumbled on my rants about farm life and thought they were funny. Thought I was funny. I'll never forget how she pitched my first book left and right while I sat at home fretting and memorizing entire sections of *Self-Publishing for Dummies*. And then, suddenly, she sold it, and my next one, too.

And now she was gone.

In the days after our conversation, I sat at my desk wondering if maybe I had nothing left to say. If maybe I'd never had anything to say. If maybe my worst fear as a writer was coming to pass: that my beloved words were joining numbers on the list of stuff at which I stink.

Stuff I Stink At:

1. Cooking.
2. Straightening my hair.
3. Math.
4. Remembering why I walked into a particular room.
5. Reading a map.
6. Have I mentioned math?

I've thought a lot about why she passed on the idea I pitched, and I've come to the following conclusion. The book I proposed wasn't a memoir. It wasn't even creative non-fiction. It was a story of how I wanted my life to be and, frankly, that's called fiction.

Two weeks after that sad chat, Cuy had a car accident.

He of the still new license was driving along one of our unlit country roads. He had the high beams on, because otherwise it's like trying to see in deep space, when suddenly he saw a car approaching. Immediately, he flipped off the high beams and not two seconds later plowed into a huge square bale of hay that probably fell off the back of somebody's pickup truck. Cuy was fine, thank God, but the hay bale destroyed the front end of the BMW and tore up the undercarriage to the tune of $7,000. Sure, I had insurance but the $1,000 deductible I owed the body shop? I also owed my landlord. Talk about lemons.

Since the bright yellow orbs wouldn't leave me alone, I decided to embrace them.

I bought a lemon-bedecked tablecloth for the kitchen, matching lemon-flecked napkins, and a package of very pretty, faux lemons I plopped in a white soup tureen and placed in the center of the table. I also added several touches of lemon yellow to our gray and white living room and decided to spread my lemon love into Cuyler's room, too. There I "decorated" with the strongest lemon-scented air fresheners I could find and yes, he was slightly offended, but only until he discovered the little satchels in his closet made his sneakers less offensive.

"Go ahead, life," my growing fondness for the sunny fruit seemed to be saying, "take your best shot. Bean me right in the kisser. But beware, I make a mean lemonade."

I've got a number of friends who joked I should throw them back and demand chocolate. Or diamonds. Or a weekend with Robert Downey Jr. But that's not how it works. Life smacks you upside the head with lemons and you don't get to say, "no thanks." You do, however, have two choices:

1. You can put them in your pocket, crawl under your desk and die stinking of rotted fruit and ruining a perfectly good pair of pants not to mention any chance of ever spending the weekend with Robert Downey Jr., or
2. You can put on your big girl panties, reach deep down inside and pull that big, fat lemon out of the hole it's left in your heart, say "You suck!" straight to its shiny rind, and go get the sugar.

It took several of those chocolate and diamond demanding girlfriends to get us into our lemon-themed space. Marina found it, Jenn handled the movers and helped me pack, and Jenn and Kim helped me unpack and put things away almost as fast as they came through the door. It was Kim though who gave me the most spot-on gift I've ever gotten: a framed, cross stitched martini glass that says,

"I'm not drunk enough for this shit." On those days the lemons leave me feeling particularly bruised, I look at it and laugh and am reminded that I'll live. After all, I've survived worse.

That little quote inspired me to fill our entry way with lots of my favorite sayings. Things like, "Life is what happens while you're busy making other plans," "Be yourself. Everyone else is already taken," and "Life doesn't have to be perfect to be wonderful."

My favorite though is the one that simply says, "When life gives you lemons, make lemonade." Every time I see it, I smile and think, my apartment is lemonade.

And you know, despite everything, it's delicious.

Bounce Boost

Sometimes at night, when my courage and confidence had the audacity to fall asleep before I did and my self-doubt got its second wind, I'd torture myself thinking about the good times. The dinner parties that ended just before breakfast. The endless rounds of Cards Against Humanity. The road trips filled with friends and the evenings spent watching movies and, God help me, Top Gear reruns until we both fell asleep on the sofa.

Those nights were hell. Morning felt years away, and self-doubt never ceased to invite second-guessing to the party it was having in my head. It was during one of those exquisitely painful trips down memory lane that I realized I had two choices: concentrate on the moments that shattered my trust in the Winemaker, or curl up next to self-doubt and worry that I threw in the towel too soon.

No way. Not doing it.

I chose to concentrate on the crap. To release the flood gates and let it rip. To relive every single second of every single stunning, out of the blue betrayal until I was so angry, I was out of bed, making coffee, and muttering like a crazy woman, *Throw in the towel? Am I insane? I clutched that towel. Cared for it. Mended the holes that man blew through it without a moment's hesitation or a morsel of remorse. I loved that towel. I didn't throw it in.*

And I didn't. I just put it down when it got too heavy and hurt too much to keep holding onto.

My last trip down memory lane was excruciating. It's awful to focus on the lemons life hits us with. But in terms of waking me up to reality and kicking both self-doubt and second-guessing out the door, I have to confess, I recommend it.

You Can Quote Me on That

I have a real thing for quotes. Almost every day I find another one (or three) that I print out and tape to the wall near my desk. I have about ten there, but my favorite is the one that simply says, "If You Can't Beat Fear, Do It Scared."

Every morning when I come into my office, those eight words are the first I read. Before I wake up my computer or read the to-do list I left myself the night before (because God knows I remember nothing these days), I look at that quote and ask myself:

Am I afraid?

If the answer is yes, I ask myself what specifically I'm afraid of.

Am I afraid of:

one child never moving out,

the other moving back in,

both children moving back in,

discovering my life insurance policy doesn't cover suicide,

getting cancer,

or getting cancer and having to count on my kids who can't get their act together enough to fly the coop to take care of me?

Of course I could be and sometimes am afraid of serious scenarios I haven't listed here, big stuff like not being able to pay my rent, buy groceries, handle (another) one of those out-of-the-blue killer car repairs, but the point is I make myself acknowledge whatever it is that's scaring me and then I ask myself the million dollar question:

If that scenario came to pass, what's the worst that could happen?

After I left the Winemaker, I was concerned about my work. I was writing about my heartbreak, the pain of getting divorced, and what it was like to start over in my mid-fifties, and I was afraid of having it published. How would people react? How would *he* react? Despite my fear, I decided that I wouldn't let it stop me. I wrote from the bottom of my heart; I wrote hoping my words might help someone else. And then I hit send, and my work was published – on one website or another – and I survived.

That fact brought me to an important conclusion, and it's simply this: a little fear is a good thing. My friend Charity's grandma always said, "Butterflies give you courage," and I think she's right. Having butterflies in your belly before an interview or presentation or audition heightens your senses and keeps you sharp. In short, a little fear of not bringing your "A" game almost guarantees you'll bring your "A" game.

If all of my worst fears came to pass tomorrow, if I couldn't pay my rent, or buy groceries, or both kids decided to cling to the coop....forever, the worst that could happen is I'd deal with it.

I don't need to beat fear because no matter what happens, I can handle it scared. You can quote me on that.

Grateful for The New Day
(No Matter How Uncertain a Day It Is)

It's gone from 75 and gorgeous to cold and blustery in Virginia and I'm trudging around the track bundled up to my eyeballs. I'm wearing a jacket, sweatshirt, wool cap, and a mask. Almost everyone I pass – keeping six feet or more away – is wearing one, too.

Walking or working out in one fashion or another is something I've done almost every day of my life. When Stu was sick, exercising kept me healthy so I could take care of him. After his death, exercising gave some structure to my days and kept the panic that raged in my brain to a low roar. It's doing the same thing now, as the death toll climbs, the economy falls further and further into the abyss, and I miss my friends and my parents, retail therapy, and blonde roots more and more each day.

The only time I didn't walk or workout every day was during my marriage to the Winemaker. My sixty minutes of me time fell by the wayside, shoved out to make time for managing personalities and tension and tempers. I spent my days in fight or flight mode, ready to play referee at the drop of a briefcase or a backpack. The results were textbook.

I gained weight. I got sick frequently. I even developed hip bursars.

"You see that?" the rheumatologist asked, circling a spot on the MRI of my lower back. "Your spine is collapsing."

I didn't ask why it was collapsing. I knew why. It was the weight of my world, all my desperate efforts to keep everything on an even keel, crushing me. And my body was crying "Uncle."

If there's anything that time in my life taught me and that I'm reminded of now when the future is so uncertain, is that keeping everything on an even keel is just not within our control. In fact, the only things within our control are our responses to people, situations, and events like economic downturns and deadly viruses.

I'm no different than anyone else; I find this situation surreal and frightening. But every day I make the choice to respond to it by taking care of my physical and mental health by walking, waving to all my fellow mask-wearing walkers, runners, cyclists, and families out with kids trying to stay sane, and being grateful for the new day no matter how uncertain a day it is.

The Bamboo Rescuer

I walk into my girlfriend's surprise fiftieth birthday party and immediately spy my friend Amy. The place is packed and though Amy is enviably petite and could hide behind a pencil, you can't miss the long thin braid that appears suddenly, as if her stylist missed a spot, from beneath the back of her shoulder length dark hair and runs down to her butt. It's not a look I could pull off, but on Amy it's too cool for school.

"The birthday girl is due shortly," she says, hugging me hello. And then, "You're awfully dressed up for a surprise party in a firehouse."

"I have to be someplace at seven," I respond.

Her eyebrows shoot up. "Care to step into my office?" she asks, nodding toward the stairs.

I follow her down and around to the back of the firehouse lest the birthday girl should arrive early, see Amy with her yellow solo cup and me sneaking a cigarette and know immediately that a) she's not needed at the firehouse party room for a neighborhood block party planning session and b) she is woefully underdressed.

"Spill it," she says, when we're safely out of sight.

"I'm meeting someone for a drink," I reply.

The someone is Robert. You might recall my mentioning him a few times earlier in this book. He is my oasis of calm, the reason I could finally, after so many years, sit down and share my story of coming full circle – sort of. I just didn't know it then.

We connected on Plenty of Fish at about the same moment I'd decided to delete my profile and take a break from dating until the turn of the next millennium. I found it exhausting and depressing: the men who communicate for days, sometimes weeks, and then completely disappear; the men who show up looking nothing like their profile pictures and get nasty when you notice; the men who communicate for days, sometimes weeks, but never ask if you'd like to meet for coffee or a cocktail. I was on POF looking for a partner in crime, not a pen pal. Why were they on? I didn't get it, any of it, and I was done.

Until I saw Robert's profile.

In one photo, he's wearing a pink dress shirt and a pair of shorts. The shirt's unbuttoned so you can't miss his awesome build, which I didn't, but honestly? He looked a little like the type of guy who goes to Polo on Friday nights, and I don't care for the guys who go to Polo on Friday nights. I need pink-shirted, fancy-shorted, overpriced-loafer-wearing "players" about as much as I need pen pals. I'm on the verge of judging a book by its cover when my eternal optimist says, "Oh hell, scroll through," and I click on another of his photos. In it, he's sitting outside someplace holding a coffee mug that says, "Home is where my Dad is." Between his tee shirt and ripped jeans, major bedhead, the five o'clock shadow that looks as if it's been five o'clock for at least a week, and the goofy smile he's giving the camera, I'm smitten. He is just so cute.

He's also out of the country, touring Paris with his daughter before dropping her off someplace else in France for school.

"But he's back now?" Amy asks.

"Got home two days ago," I reply.

"He can't really live here in Marshall," Amy says. "There *are* no handsome, single men who live in Marshall."

"Maybe he's full of it," I reply. "Wouldn't be the first time."

I glance at my phone. It's five to seven. I'm meeting Robert at Field and Main restaurant which is sixty whole seconds from the firehouse.

"Have a good time," Amy says, hugging me.

"My guess is I'll be on my way home by eight," I reply, smiling.

As it turns out, it was a surprisingly good guess. And I was only off by twelve hours.

****

I park, check my lip gloss, and think *If this guy doesn't look like his pictures, I'm suing the people at Plenty of Fish. And whoever invented Internet dating. And Al Gore for inventing the Internet. And global warming 'cause I'm starting to sweat, and I think that's his sin, too.* Then I hop out, round the corner, and striding toward me is this tall, dark-haired, broad shouldered, lanky, long-legged dream. In his dark jeans, three buttons open at the collar, untucked, slightly fitted, long-sleeved button-down shirt in a mix of pastel pinks and purples, he looks like the love child of GQ and J Crew. He cannot possibly be the man *I'm* meeting for a drink. But maybe he is because he gives me a wave, takes my hand, and says, oh hell I don't remember what he said. All I remember is that whatever he said, he said it with a twang and all I could think was *Oh dear God, tall, dark, and lanky is from Texas. I'm in trouble.*

****

Sometimes when I meet new people, they tell me they could listen to me talk all day. This horrifies me as I know how awful my Jersey honk is. But sitting across from Robert at a table upstairs in the bar, I finally understood where those folks were coming from. I could have listened to him all night. And so, I did. Over one glass of wine, then a second, a third complemented by an enormous steak that we split, then another couple of glasses back at his house, by the pool, under twinkling white lights as music wafted from the cabana. At some point I realized it was late, really late, and I should go home. But when I stood up to leave, I discovered I couldn't feel my feet. He'd swept me completely off them. So, I stayed.

I told Amy I'd probably be on my way home by eight, I just neglected to add "in the morning."

****

I am the eldest of four, Robert is the youngest of four. I had three younger brothers; he has three older sisters. I am used to being the boss, he is used to being the prince. During our first year together, I threw him a small birthday dinner and arranged to have Jenn make him the cake his mom always made for him. I got the recipe from his sister Connie. I was so excited. He would be so surprised!

The dinner party was lovely. The cake came out great. It was only when he cut it, and put it on the plate I was holding, and I turned and gave the first piece to a guest that things went awry. In Robert's family, the birthday boy or girl gets the first slice. In my family, the first slice is given to a guest as are all subsequent slices until only the birthday boy or girl is left. Then they get cake.

The birthday boy looked at me with hurt puppy eyes that said *How could you give away my cake?* And I looked back at him with a righteous, big sister glare that said *How could you be so impolite to our guests?*

The rest of the evening didn't go too well, and, in the morning, I did what I always do when I'm hurt and angry. I called my mom.

Sue, are you telling me that you and Robert got into a tiff over a piece of birthday cake?

Me, sniffling, *yes.*

And you're crying over this tiff over a piece of birthday cake?

Me, still sniffling, *yes.*

You both need to grow up.

****

One Sunday morning sometime in our second year of dating and eons before the coronavirus, I'm on the lanai having coffee when Robert comes out. He's wearing a tee shirt, running shorts, and sneakers. I had no idea he owned sneakers. I'd seen his snakeskin boots and his collection of shoes that rival a DSW and make mine look like I failed girl school, but these style-challenged white things surprised me.

"Whatcha doing?" I ask.

"Going for a run," he replies.

"At the track?"

"No," he replies pointing to the street, "right here."

"Along the road?" People, chickens, ducks, and cows take their lives in their hands everyday crossing or just walking along the side of our section of Rectortown Road. "But it's not safe!"

"It's fine. I go a little past the railroad tracks and turn around," he says kissing me. "I'll be right back."

He takes off and I walk to the end of the driveway to watch him go.

Then I wait.

Five minutes becomes twenty minutes. It's sunny and hot and I hate the heat almost as much as I hate that he's running along Virginia's version of the autobahn. Worry wart that I am, I decide to get my car keys just in case I have to go look for him.

I walk inside, grab my bag, and hear his pickup truck start.

What the—?

I look and Robert's in the truck, backing out of the driveway and racing off in the direction of the railroad tracks. Is he off to rescue a runner he's found mushed on the side of the road? I'll bet he is. I'm certain he is! See? I knew it was unsafe! Maybe next time he'll go to the track. The track is much safer. It won't stop you from getting laid off, but at least you're not going to get hit by a tractor or a cattle carrier.

Once again I'm standing near the end of our driveway waiting and worrying. Ten minutes becomes twenty minutes. Twenty minutes become a half an hour. Is the runner dead? Is Robert ok? Maybe I should call 911. I call Robert. No answer. I text him. No reply. My face is in my phone, calling him again, when I realize he's pulling in next to me. And hopping out of the truck. And completely covered in dirt.

Dirt. But not blood.

"What happened?" I ask, feeling the urge to simultaneously faint with relief and smack him for scaring me. "Is everything ok? I was worried!"

"I was worried too," he says reaching into the bed of the pickup and pulling an enormous plant, the roots of which look as if they've been ripped from the earth in a frenzy, toward him. "I was worried about this!"

"And what is that?"

"It's bamboo," he replies like I should know. "It was growing right out into the road from someone's property!"

"So you stole it?"

"No," he replies, looking at me indignantly. "I—" he pauses, and I can see the wheels turning. "I rescued it! It could have been killed!"

Of course, he rescued it. That's how Robert is. I should know. He rescued me.

****

At this writing, the bamboo rescuer and I have been together almost three years and have lived together eight months. I'm happy we didn't rush to make my toothbrush (and the millions of overpriced concoctions I use in a never-ending quest to stop my face from falling because indeed, it is falling) a permanent fixture in his bathroom. It gave us time to really get to know each other, to discover that we travel well together (he likes to fly, I'm ok with it. He prefers the window seat, I prefer to forget I'm anywhere near a window), survive each other's colds (we're excellent at taking care of each other although as soon as I'm done sniffling I want kisses and he's like, *Whoa matey! Let's wait another week!),* enjoy our respective birthdays our way (he gets the first piece of birthday cake, I get the last, and we laugh), and fall in love with each other's families.

Of course what I didn't know about him is his talent for going into survivalist mode.

We were in San Diego early in March when suddenly the talk at every restaurant we went to turned to cancellations at the convention center. The bartenders and waitstaff were abuzz with bad news. Events that drew twenty-thousand, thirty-thousand people annually were being cancelled left and right. Hotels, restaurants, and shops that counted on that business were on the brink of a very bad time.

And then Cuyler called me.

He was playing in a rugby tournament in Toronto. "Mom," he said, "we all have to go home. And then we have to quarantine. What the hell is going on?"

What was going on is what's still going on. The Coronavirus. COVID-19. The pandemic. Robert and I flew home, him in his window seat, me pretending planes don't have windows, and both of us trying not to breathe in the air that might or might not contain particles of a deadly disease we didn't, and still don't, understand. Cuy flew home, went straight to the house he shares with a few teammates at Mount St. Mary's University, and locked himself in his room. Friends brought him food. Robert and I ventured out to the supermarket to discover there was no food. Not fresh, not frozen, nothing. And forget finding toilet paper.

That's when my man burst into survivalist mode.

Suddenly the freezer in the basement that had never been plugged in was plugged in, and cleaned, and stocked with whatever he could find from trips he made to supermarkets all across the state. Meat, chicken, fish, vegetables; if he found it, he froze it. He stocked the kitchen cabinets to bursting too and then?

Then he turned his attention to the chicken coop.

I didn't even know we had a chicken coop.

I might not have moved in – or hell, dated him – if I had. The hens and I were never on friendly terms when I lived on the farm and I have a scar on my scalp to prove it.

Dear God, we have a chicken coop. And now, of course, we have chickens. And eggs that they like to lay around our spectacularly beautiful inground pool. And the laughter you hear? Is Stu, howling hysterically at me from Heaven.

Dear God. I've gone full circle. Sort of.

Losing Wendy

She was a rugby mom like the rest of us. She stood on the sidelines watching her son the same way the rest of us watched our sons – hands over our eyes, fingers parted just enough to be able to see. Rugby is so tough – as evidenced by the sport's tagline "No helmets. No pads. Just balls." – that it's nothing short of terrifying to watch the child you've spent your life protecting hit that pitch and the opposing team unprotected. Maybe it's different for dads, but for moms, that fear bonds us.

None of us knew Wendy that well but, huddled next to each other (and occasionally hiding behind each other's backs when the fingers over the eyes thing wasn't cutting it), united in pride for our sons ("Go Doug! Go Mikey!"), fear they'd get hurt ("Who's down? Is that Will? Cuyler?"), and the delectable Bloody Mary's Robert whipped up and served surreptitiously (shhhh), we were the Mount Saint Mary's University Men's Rugby moms. More importantly, we were friends.

And then she got sick.

Esophageal cancer.

At a match shortly after her diagnosis, Wendy turned to Coco, our fearless and hysterically funny head rugby mom whose husband coached all our kids until, surprisingly and not so surprisingly, they each ended up playing for Mount St Mary's and said, *All I want is to see Doug graduate.*

She got sicker and we didn't see her for a long while. A few of us tried to visit but, God bless her husband, when he felt Wendy needed rest, no one was allowed in. I don't blame him one bit; he knew we'd hide our Bloody Mary fixins and snacks under our coats and in our bags and tucked in our bras and then God only knows what kind of rugby mom mayhem would have ensued. But then one Saturday, out of the blue, Wendy was there, at a match, not just cheering the boys on, but having made the most delicious Chinese food for them to enjoy (and us to sneak tastes of).

Wendy was Chinese, her husband Irish, their sons kind and good looking as the day is long.

It wasn't but a few weeks after that Saturday that she went into the hospital for the last time. Her son Doug came home from the Mount. His best friend Will did too. Doug, Will, Coco, all of Wendy's dearest friends, her husband Steve, their older son Steven, converged in her hospital room. Steve wanted Wendy to rest. He wanted her to be done with the pain and to be able to let go in peace without others around her crying, praying, and holding on. I wasn't there, but I heard. Steve wanted Wendy to go unencumbered. Yet no one would leave.

At two o'clock on a Friday afternoon, I got a text from Coco. Beautiful, loving, effervescent, petite-as-my-pinky but larger-than-life Wendy was gone.

My heart broke then, and it breaks now writing about it. Wendy was light, and joy, and goodness, and she was so damn funny. She adored her sons and when she looked at Steve, you could see that even after all their years together, she was still smitten with him. She loved us rugby moms and we loved her. And now, she's gone. Taken by cancer too fast, too soon, too young.

Obviously, I've experienced loss. Painful, heart wrenching, terrible loss. Loss that was expected, and loss that came out of the clear blue sky, and I still can't believe that I'll never see Wendy again. She'll never again hide behind me on the sidelines, giggling and watching Doug through her fingers right up until the moment he'd catch that ball like his hands were made of glue and take off down the field for the try. You should've seen her then, racing down the sideline with him, screaming her support, watching her baby score.

I will never see her do that again and, far worse, neither will her husband and sons.

I just don't get it. There are so may truly terrible people in this world that – forgive me – deserve truly terrible deaths.

But Wendy? Stu? What could possibly be the reason for their lives to be cut short?

There is no reason. In some cosmic spot they rolled the dice and Wendy lost. Stu and David lost, too. Victims don't get to sit at the table and place their bets. The game is going on someplace else without them.

How long before the cosmos plays the hand that determines my fate?

Wendy, I'm so sorry we never got to know each other better, beyond the rugby sidelines, but I want you to know that I loved you. All the Mount St. Mary's University Men's Rugby moms loved you. Now and forever, you have my word, when we're watching the boys through our fingers, you'll be in our hearts (which, frankly, might be a safer place to watch from), and when your baby gets the ball and he's flying down the field to score, we'll be running along the sidelines with him, screaming your support.

Getting Through It

If I'm walking on the track, in the car on my way to the track, or lacing up my sneakers and digging out my keys to drive to the track, my boss calls. I'm unsure what that's about but I can tell you this: if I skip a day and don't go to the track? I don't hear from him. Since I've been worried for a while now that when he calls it'll be to tell me the magazines I edit are folding and therefore I'm completely out of a job, I frequently consider giving up my trips to the track altogether. But I can't. When Robert has the crock pot going in the kitchen (as he usually does) and the aroma wafts my way, it's so hard not to give in and dig in. All the way in. To the point where the answer to "What's for dinner?" really is DiGiorno.

This morning, I'm sitting on the lanai watching a Cardinal watch me. I've got my sneakers on but what I really want is more coffee and maybe a nap. That thought propels me to my feet and my phone rings.

Of course it does.

"Hey Bruce," I answer, "how are you?"

He says he's fine and then, as he does every time, he asks after Casey and Cuyler, after Robert, and after me. I have been blessed to work for several terrific publishers in my life, and Bruce is one of them. He's a real journalist, The Washington Post, New York Times kind, and he's taught me so much. I enjoy working with him too, except for maybe that one day when he called and asked if I'd set up a budget yet and I thought, *Oh holy Hell. I need to do math?* (He didn't mean that kind of budget, thank God.) The other thing that I really appreciate about him is that he asks how *my* work is going. How many managers do you know who genuinely support their employee's side hustle? Not many. He's supportive of my writing and, when I relaunched my speaking career with my first TED talk, he and his wife came to cheer me on.

"We'd like you to come back to work on Monday," he says. "Sound good?"

"Sounds great!" I reply, doing a little happy dance and barely registering the rest of what he's saying, something about thirty-two as opposed to forty hours a week, and a commensurate pay cut, and, and, honestly? I don't care. I'm going back to work!

Robert's at his desk when I burst through the door and announce, "I go back to work Monday!"

"That's great, babe," he replies, smiling. And then, "We're getting through this."

****

We *are* getting through this, I think, adjusting my mask and pulling my black wool cap down to help keep the band over my ears and my headphones in them. I'm walking as fast as I can to try and compensate for making too many visits to the crockpot and to keep warm. My fingers are freezing, and my nose is running. Is Virginia always this cold in April? I can't recall. I'm also unsure how close we are to coming out the other side of this thing, but progress, no matter how small, is still progress. I have my job back. I have a beautiful man in my life whom I love. Our kids, his daughter, and my boys, are healthy. I'm so thankful, I blow a gratitude gasket and burst into tears right there on the track.

You can probably imagine what a mess I made of my mask.

Put It Out There

As I've mentioned, too often we carry around a dream or goal that feels huge and unattainable to us, so huge we convince ourselves that we can never achieve it because we don't have what it takes. We tell no one about this dream until one day, a situation arises, and we blurt it out, embarrassed to have such lofty aspirations. We wait for a laugh or a snarky response and instead we get support. Encouragement. Suddenly the dream doesn't feel so farfetched. Emboldened, we begin to share it with others and our dream is launched into the world where God, the energy of the Universe, the Cosmos, picks it up and conspires to bring it to us.

I've told you about my dream of being an editor, but I had another that I kept to myself until, believe it or not, the height of the "bucket list" craze.

One afternoon, a group of my girlfriends were sharing the things they most want to do before they die. I didn't want them to ask me, and yet I did. I really did. I longed to tell someone about this "thing" I was carrying, even if it was just to make it go away.

Finally, one of them asked me.

"I want to see the Amalfi coast," I blurted. "But what I really, really, really want is to give a TED Talk."

I waited for a giggle, or a snarky, "Oh, so now you think you're Brené Brown, do you?" I didn't get it.

"You'd be wonderful!" is what I got.

"You should do that! You're a great speaker!" is what I got.

"Who do we know that can help you do that?" is what I got.

I should have known it would go this way. These were my friends, after all. How could I not have trusted them sooner with what was in my heart?

In sharing my dream, I released it to the Universe and the Universe laced up its sneakers and ran with it.

A short time later, I had to select a nonprofit to spotlight in the business magazine I edit. Bruce suggested TEDx Tysons and, without giving it a second thought, I assigned the feature to Jenn who, in addition to being one of my best friends, is one of the best writers I've ever worked with. She conducted the interview, wrote the story, got the photos and sent everything to me.

I read it. Loved it. Didn't change a sentence and sent it to layout.

Two weeks later, she arrives for ladies' night at my house. Before she'd even taken off her coat, she shot me a look and said, "So?"

"What?" I replied.

"The piece. Did you read it?" She asked.

"Of course, I read it. It's great. All your work is great. That's why I pay you the big bucks!" I laughed.

She didn't.

"If you read it," she continued, "then you know about the open mic competition."

Indeed, I knew about it. They were inviting people to compete for a spot in the next TEDx Tysons event.

"You have to enter," she said, taking the wine bottle from me before I, as usual, had the chance to destroy the cork. "This is your bucket list wish! Come on. You'll win."

Frankly, I wasn't sure, but I wanted the chance so badly, I put aside my fear of making a fool of myself and entered. I submitted my bio, my list of previous speaking engagements, and the idea for my talk.

They liked my idea. I was invited to compete. I didn't know what to do first – faint or phone my mom.

Robert and I arrived at the Alden Theatre the night of the competition. I took my seat among the forty-nine other hopefuls and crossed my fingers. Twenty-five of us would be selected at random to give a three-minute pitch to the panel of judges. The remaining twenty-five would get just one minute. I wasn't nervous. I was ready. More importantly, I was grateful – to God, the Universe, and Jenn for putting this chance in my path.

And I'll tell you something else: I knew that if my name was pulled to give my pitch, I'd win.

They pulled my name.

I made my pitch.

I won.

Put it out there.

I have a confession to make

We're out of toilet paper.

I've spent my entire life battling IBS with constipation and now? Now that such an affliction would work in my favor? Forget it.

Up until the start of the pandemic and the disappearance of every single solitary paper product from the shelves of every single solitary supermarket, I thought that finally being regular rocked. Now I'm like, "Oh, IBS-C, where doth thou be?"

It's OK though. We've still got tissues, plenty of them, and that's not including the handfuls I use to stuff my bra. And no, I'm definitely not dipping into those. When we're out of Kleenex we can move on to magazines, newspapers, paper bags, dryer sheets, and sales receipts. Sorry, but there's no way I'm screwing with my cup size for the sake of "down south."

Even in these uncertain times, a girl's got to have her priorities.

In fact, right now it's more important than ever to hold fast to what matters to us: our kids, significant others, extended family and friends, our work, the organizations we support, our hobbies, and our um, interesting habits...

So please, don't tell Robert I'm stockpiling Kleenex. He's already wondering why I'm saving sales receipts.

Be the Person You'd Want to be Quarantined With

Snow days. Rainy days. Days so cold and blustery the only thing to do is light a fire, wrap yourself in a blanket and read a book. Those once-in-awhile breaks are welcome and peaceful.

Being locked down in one's house however, with the kids and your significant other while one or both of you are trying to work and trying not to worry if at the end of this you'll have work, is another thing entirely. It'll make you antsy, short-tempered, snappish, and worse.

Being stuck inside the house can quickly become being stuck inside our heads, and we all know what happens then. Our anxiety runs amok, conjuring up the worst possible scenarios and in no time, we're watching our terrifying fate play out on the big screen in our skull. Even worse? There's no movie popcorn and my part isn't played by Reese Witherspoon.

Don't be this person. It's unhealthy, unfair, and downright damaging to you, and to all those you're quarantined with.

Instead, be the person you'd want to be quarantined with. The person who steers clear of the rabbit hole and keeps others from falling into the abyss, too. Here's how.

You are what you think

"Life is not always a matter of holding good cards, but sometimes playing a poor hand well." Jack London

Right now, it seems we've all been dealt a poor hand, but it's our call as to how we think about the cards we're clutching and how we play them. If we choose to think of them as lousy, well, what can you do with lousy cards? Nothing. Might as well fold. But if instead we think of them as interesting options to be explored, we become energized, excited. Our creative juices start flowing, our endorphins start firing. Suddenly we've taken back some control and now we're in the driver's seat. And who doesn't love being in the driver's seat, calling the shots, and maybe getting to cast Reese Witherspoon in one's blockbuster biopic?

Find the humor

"If you can't make it better, you can laugh at it." Erma Bombeck

You're out of printer paper, the lyrics to Let it Go are burned into your brain, and you're starting to appreciate why some animals eat their young when it happens. You discover your eight-year-old niece using your laptop. You race toward her, but it's too late. She's already hit "reply all" and told your staff (and your boss), "Aunt Susan's in the bathroom. She might be awhile. This is Makenna."

You've got to laugh. After you're done crying, of course.

Practice gratitude

"Enjoy the little things, for one day you may look back and realize they were the big things." Robert Brault

Every time you wash your hands, scrub down a countertop, or step outside for a moment to get some air and/or bring in the groceries some brave soul delivered, think of three things you're grateful for. The brave soul who brought the food; your health; your kids' health; your stockpile of black yoga pants; Facetime and Zoom so you can see your folks and they can see your kids because, let's face it, the little buggers responsible for Let it Go being burned into your brain and the people you work with being concerned you're constipated, are all they care about. And that's another thing to be grateful for.

Yes, we're living in uncertain times, but aren't we always? There's never been a time when we've been in complete control of our circumstances, but we have always been and always will be in control of how we respond to them.

So, respond like the person you'd want to be quarantined with would respond.

Laugh at every possible opportunity. Be grateful for every single solitary good thing in your life. And steer clear of the rabbit hole. Last I checked, there was still no movie popcorn and Reese Witherspoon still refused to play me.

Just Another Blue-gened Girl

Right this moment, Robert is sitting on the lanai taking a break from cutting the lawn. It's absolutely beautiful out. Sunny, crisp, breezy; a welcome break from the blistering heat that descended as if on a mission to make us all regret our complaints about the cold. He's called me to join him, but I'm dawdling. I've got my coffee, a box of Kleenex, and an old tape playing in my head.

Dammit Susan, dammit Susan, dammit. Normal people do not need tissues to cope with a cloudless blue sky.

I should be used to it by now, my body's occasional, painful, response to the type of day that makes others feel like going for a run, playing catch with their kids, sitting outside with their significant other.

Sometimes I see it coming. Other times it takes me by surprise. Like this morning.

I stepped outside to go to the track, mentally daring my boss to buzz me and expecting to find more of the mugginess we've had lately. But no; the weather had broken. A blanket of lemon-yellow sunshine covered the garden, and the breeze smelled sweet, tinged with a bouquet of hydrangea, and sleeping wisteria.

In an instant, the scent, and the brush of the cool air on my arms, sickened me to my stomach.

Obviously, it's not the response most people have to such a day, particularly a spring-like day in the middle of summer, but every once in a while it's how it is for me. And once I'm nauseous, it's no time before panic makes an appearance and my arms begin a kind of electrical storm that surges from my biceps to the tips of my fingers and back again, and that completes the trifecta of symptoms that commence my descent down the rabbit hole.

"Down the rabbit hole;" my absolute favorite euphemism for "Shit, my depression's at DEFCON 4."

Having gone through these episodes most of my life, I know that if I gave in and let it rip, sat down and cried like someone stole my favorite Kate Spade bag, the entire thing might move faster. But I can't. I just can't bring myself to simply roll over and capitulate to feeling like crap. Instead, I wield my mouth, say something sarcastic, and fight like hell to corral the big, bad, blues into the tiny box I imagine I keep in my belly. Sure, sarcasm is funny. But it's also a form of anger. And anger is very often a defense mechanism.

And I, my friends, am the defense department.

Honest as I am about my depression, which for me is like a constant low tide, lapping at the shores of my serotonin stores, there are just times I don't want to deal with it. I want it to go away. I want to stamp my feet and shout "No fair! I haven't missed my meds in ages!" I honestly want to throw a tantrum, but to tell you the truth? I don't have the energy.

One minute, I'm fine. Just going about my business. Checking email, jotting work notes I'll need later on. One minute, my future is as bright as anybody else's. The next, I have no future. Suddenly, and like today, quite literally out of the God-it's-good-to-be-alive blue sky, everything feels futile. Pointless. Like I'm pushing a boulder up a hill and, well, why bother? It will never get any easier. I will always feel this empty, hopeless, and exhausted. Why not just stop, let that big ass rock roll back onto me, and be done with it?

There are those who would look at me at this moment and demand I pull myself up by my bootstraps, buck up, and knock off the pity party. In response, I'll simply say this: the sense of desperation and melancholy that engulfs me and, dare I say, others, when depression strikes, is no party. If it were, don't you think we'd have taken ourselves off the guest list a long time ago?

It's those same people who are the first ones to whisper, "Why the hell does she even talk about this stuff?" I talk about "this stuff" because it's the only way I can get a foothold in the rabbit hole and begin the climb up and out. I talk because there are people out there who need to and won't because they think they're alone. That no one will understand. That this is just their lot in life, so the best they can do is to learn to deal.

I talk because silence kills. And I mean living death as much as I do suicide.

Several years ago, I was having lunch with one of my dearest friends. We're both Jersey girls, transplanted to Virginia. We sat there talking kids and work, and how much exercise we were (and weren't) getting. We talked hair and nails, the great buys we found at

Marshall's, aging parents and travel plans we hoped would come to fruition. We probably spent close to two hours catching up, and the entire time I had the sense that there was something she wasn't saying. Something she couldn't quite decide if she wanted to get off her chest.

Until the waitress dropped the check.

We reached for it at the same time and she said, no, stop, my treat. I made some comment about it not being my birthday and let's split it and don't be silly, sister. But she wasn't having any of it.

"It's my treat," she said, "to thank you for that article." I had no idea what she was talking about. "The one, you know, about the rabbit hole."

A few weeks earlier, a column I'd written which I actually called *Down the Rabbit Hole*, ran in the local paper. It was the first essay I'd ever done about my depression. It wasn't the usual fluffy, funny stuff, I contributed. Rather it was a piece that just poured out of me one morning when I woke up and realized I was finally, mercifully back from the abyss.

Well, at least now I knew what we weren't discussing over our chicken Caesar salads.

"You know, Suz," she continued, "I had no idea. And I feel bad about that. But, and please don't take this the wrong way, it was such a relief. To find out that even my friend, the peppy blonde, gets the blues."

Over one more hour, two more cups of coffee, and the dessert we originally declined but then went ahead and ordered anyway, (I mean, hell, she was paying), she told me how she'd been feeling and how she'd kept it to herself. My piece, she said, kind of gave her permission to speak up. She figured if I could do it in public, she could be brave and do it in private. She shared the column with her husband and leveled with him. The next day she made an appointment to see her doctor.

I could hardly believe it. I'd had so many concerns about that piece, about "coming out" in such a small community. But as she talked, they evaporated. If five hundred words had helped just one person, I'd done the right thing.

But that was then. And this, as they say, is now.

"Babe! It's beautiful out here!" Rob's usually up and back at 'em by now, watering, pulling weeds, hauling ass on the riding mower like it's a race car, but no, he's waiting for me, hoping to get his vampire-like girlfriend to venture out into the light. I, however, would prefer to hide here, at my desk, pretending to write and feeling awful about feeling awful. I can stuff it, and hope it goes away. But that's just delaying the inevitable. I step out onto the lanai and put my tissues on the table.

"Rabbit hole, huh?"

I nod, and he takes my hand. We watch several brave souls out for a jog, and several equally brave ducks waddle their way across the street to our front yard.

"Good to see Marge and the girls," I say.

"Good to have you out here," he replies.

I watch the hens try to escape the backyard and the ducks make their way to Rob's putting green. I can hear our neighbors, Charity and Chris, laughing as they stow their kayaks for a day on the river and watch as a mass of cyclists careen down Rectortown Road. I should make myself take the walk I skipped this morning. Or at least throw in a load of laundry. But both thoughts exhaust me; it was all I could do to get out here.

"I know what'll make you feel better," Robert says suddenly. "We'll watch golf!"

I laugh and snort at the same time. "There is no golf, silly. Besides, it's Saturday."

"Details, details," he says, squeezing my hand. And then, "You know you'll feel better if you cry."

I love this man. Most men would sooner be sentenced to spend the rest of their life without sex than encourage a woman to cry. But my sweet bamboo rescuer is not most men.

His kindness cracks me open and I give in. I cry and rant about how stupid it is to be crying. How I know it will pass but why does it have to happen in the first place? He doesn't say too much. Mostly, he listens. Hands me tissues. Runs his fingers through my hair. It doesn't make it better. But it does make it bearable. And because I can talk with him, I can see the light, at the top of the rabbit hole, and begin the climb out.

■■■

****

****

Top 3 Things I've Learned in the Last 5 Days ...

3.

I've learned that when Cuy is in a relationship, hearing about its ups and downs sends my empathy into overdrive and in no time my heart is breaking as if my own relationship is in such turmoil. I take on his pain and walk around in his fog and heartache. And what good is that? It doesn't ease his suffering and it exhausts me. Empathy is good. Putting yourself in someone else's shoes is good. But lacing them up and running around in them is insanity.

2.

I've learned that even though Casey continues to excel in ways we never dreamt possible, spending time with him requires an exceptional amount of energy. And I've learned that I don't have an exceptional amount of energy anymore. Which means no more spur of the moment visits. Dates with him need to be made in advance and the night before I see him, I need sleep. Lots of sleep. The day of, I need a nap. He needs me at my best, my most patient. And I need to have the energy to wrestle his runaway train of a brain out of the rabbit hole and toward the nearest sign of light.

1.

I've learned that if I don't put the brakes on the emotional energy I put into both my sons, I will cry. A lot. Sometimes non-stop.

Learning these things of late has reminded me of lessons I learned long ago. Things like when I hop out of bed at four in the morning and whirl from writing to ironing to painting trim to stenciling a floor, there is something I don't want to think about. And that not thinking about the something I don't want to think about will make me think, *why am I crying?*

I've also learned that the answer, at least today, is that I'm caught up in both my kids' "stuff," I'm tired, and I've stenciled myself out of the bathroom which is where my makeup is and that means I can't fix the mess I've made of my face.

And I've learned that I'm probably going to live because that thought? Made me laugh.

****

****

Bounce Boost

Never in my life did I envision a day when I'd conference with my coworkers via video looking professional from the waist up and homeless from the waist down, decide in March that the only Christmas gift worth discovering under the tree is toilet paper, or find myself on a quest for face masks and matching gloves. Which also would make nice gifts, now that I think of it.

Never in my life did I think I'd be consumed with worry that the people I love will get sick, be sick with longing to see them (and be permitted to hug them), and obsessed with finding a way to make the six-hour drive from Virginia to New Jersey without having to stop to use a public restroom. I guess I could rent an RV but that's a pretty penny and with my pay cut I just don't have that many pennies these days. I could go the adult diaper route but the thought of being stopped for whatever and possibly being told to step out of the car while looking like a female Baby Huey would put me in a psych ward. No doubt next to the cop who stopped me. I've even considered making the entire trip without consuming any kind of liquid but worry I'd arrive dehydrated, delirious, and forced to make a detour to the emergency room. Which of course is better than the psych ward but not by much.

Never in my life did I think I'd be told to stay home, then told it's ok to go out – but only if I stay six-feet away from anyone I encounter and only if I wear the aforementioned face mask (and matching gloves if I can find them) – and realize I don't like being told what to do particularly by people who clearly don't know what to do.

And never in my life did I think that if a situation such as we're in occurred, and the doctors and scientists and researchers and politicians didn't have a handle on it, that my reaction would be to pray for them.

But I'm older now.

I've lived through a lot.

And I know that the people we count on to steer the ship through the storm are just that – people. And so I pray for them.

Never in my life did I think I'd be so mature and so immature at the same time. Because you *know* that while I'm praying, I'm still wondering how best to get to New Jersey. And at this moment, I'm leaning heavily toward the female Baby Huey business. But only if I pair it with a Prozac.

There's a Bear by the Pool

It's half an hour until wine time on Saturday afternoon and I'm in the sunroom curled up on one of our bright yellow recliners, desperate to finish the last few pages of Liane Moriarity's *The Hypnotist's Love Story*. I've been hypnotized by all its pages and now, approaching the end, the final words, the "what a great book!" moment, I'm in a trance. Totally absorbed. I've loved this book and learned from it, too. In fact, I plan to hypnotize Robert when we go to bed. I wanted to practice on him earlier, but he's been cleaning the pool and working in the garden all day (aka, ducking me). I'm unsure what I plan to achieve by hypnotizing him, but I'm leaning toward convincing him to rub my feet. They're hideous, and I've seen pedicurists blanche at the sight of my misshapen big toes and multiple missing nails, but still. Diamonds and foot rubs are a girl's best friends.

I'm so absorbed, I hear nothing. See nothing but the words on the page. I've got to get to the end before I'm late for cocktail hour and Robert starts wondering if I'm running a fever or something.

I flip to the second to last page barely able to breathe. Here it comes, the finale, the answer to my many questions. I'm *thisclose* when the sound of scuffling interrupts my reverie. I turn and behind me, on the lanai, are our neighbors Chris and Charity. Charity looks startled. Chris is staring intently into the backyard. I wave for them to come in, but they stand there. I try to quickly unfurl myself, but my legs and feet are asleep and in two seconds I've got toe cramps so bad I'm crying and limping my way to the door. I figure they're early for wine. No problem. I can ask Charity to pour while I duck into the bathroom to press my toes into the cold tile and, of course, quickly finish my book.

"Hi guys," I say, opening the door, "come on in!"

No one moves so I wince my way outside.

"What's up?" I ask, as their 16-year-old son Joel rounds the corner and announces, "Mr. McCord just texted dad that there's a bear by the pool!"

How can there be a bear by the pool? The backyard is completely fenced in. But if there *is* a bear by the pool, this could be the perfect opportunity to try out my new hypnotherapy skills! I could put the bear in a trance, we could shoot it with a tranquilizer dart (surely somebody around here has a tranquilizer dart, we live in the country for Pete's sake), and then the authorities could come and take the bear home to, well, wherever the bear lives. I'm clutching my book to my chest, completely absorbed in my brilliant idea, when suddenly it dawns on me, I should be worried about Robert (aka Mr. McCord). He's at the pool with a bear!

"Is Robert ok?" I ask.

Chris and Charity say nothing. Joel shrugs.

"Ok, here's the plan," start. "I'm going to hypnotize the bear—"

"Hypnotize the—?" Joel says, cutting me off, his saucer size eyes soaring to dinner plate status.

"Yes," I reply excitedly, holding out the book. "I just read this! I can do it!"

The three of them look at me like either I've lost it, or I launched into wine time early.

I look at Chris, whose eyes are the size of his son's. "Once the bear is in a trance, we're going to need a tranquilizer dart. Do you have one?" I pause and look at Charity. "Maybe one of the neighbors has one?"

"A tranquilizer dart?" Charity asks incredulously and then, turning to Chris, "Give me that phone!"

Chris hands over his phone.

Charity looks at it once, then twice, and laughs.

"Chris," she says, "there's *beer* by the pool! *Beer*, not bear!"

"Oops. Read it too fast," Chris smiles sheepishly.

"He's dyslexic," Charity offers.

"I'm disappointed," I confess.

Chris and Joel look at me like *are you kidding?* and take off to the backyard. Chris to visit with Robert and the beer by the pool. Joel just to jump in.

"That book's gone to your head," Charity laughs when they're out of earshot.

"Yeah well, I was hoping it would go to my feet," I reply.

"Not gonna happen," she replies, knowing immediately what I had in mind because she was there pre-COVID when the pedicurist saw my feet and the salon owner almost had to call the paramedics. "You're gonna need a whole lot more than hypnotism to get Rob to rub those puppies!"

A girl can dream, right?

And a girl can go finish her book. Which is what I did, snapping it closed just as Robert got out the corkscrew.

Crazy as it sounds, I'd still like to test my hypnotherapy skills. And if salons ever open again, I know a lovely but traumatized nail tech who might even let me.

Epilogue

"Mom, I need money for books." It's Cuy, and today is the first day of his senior year at the Mount. He has one class he has to take in person, the rest are online, and it's the first time in four years there's no fall rugby season. "I'll send it to you if you promise to put some of it toward masks and actually wear one," I reply. He laughs and says he will. But I know he won't. I worry constantly that he'll get sick and wind up in the hospital.

Casey calls too, to tell me he's been promoted. Now he's the lead host at the restaurant he's working at. I'm not surprised and of course I'm proud of him, but I'm petrified too. His managers love him because he's the only host who'll go toe to toe with customers who try to enter without wearing a mask. The incidents he tells me about scare the daylights out of me. I worry constantly that someone will pop him, and he'll wind up in the hospital.

I can't get one to wear a mask, and I can't get the other to call a manager when a customer won't comply with wearing a mask. I could stand this whole COVID thing better if my kids would just listen to me.

"We are powerless to protect the people we love," my mom says when I call her later in the day. She's right, and I love her, and I hate that I haven't seen her in so long. I haven't seen my dad or my brother, Nick, all of whom live in New Jersey, either. (The adult diaper and a Prozac approach still appeals to me, but driving Depens-ed and medicated, mostly medicated, might not be the best way to go.)

At the moment it's sunny and cool, and not pouring. For the last two weeks we've had several soaking storms that I can only thank God for. Robert did some serious damage to his back right before the rains came and has been in bed ever since. Without the downpours we've gotten almost every day, his vegetable garden, fruit trees, crazy tall patches of the bamboo he rescued, and all the landscaping he's done around the pool including the banana trees which are indescribably gorgeous, would be dead. As I've already watched a man I loved watch his garden die, you can imagine how thankful I am that the more it rains, the more Rob can rest and heal without worrying.

I realize you might be thinking, *Hey Suz, you're an able-bodied gal. If it doesn't rain, get out there and water!* And I can, and I will, but that's not something you want me doing. Stu used to call me "Black Thumbed Thusie" because no matter what I did or tried to be helpful with, the plant, bush, or bulb died. That, or it committed suicide at the sight of me in my gardening gloves coming to fill in for the real McCoy or McCorkindale or, in this case, McCord. Trust me, Stu didn't want my help and I know Robert doesn't either.

Nine years since his death, I can tell you there isn't a moment that goes by that I don't feel Stu with me. We'd known each other thirty-two years when cancer took him. He was my hero and my champion. He taught me how to negotiate, helped me build the confidence to leave corporate America and establish myself first as a copywriter and then as an author. When I had doubts, he had faith. And when I started to see some success – landed the client, got the publishing contract, booked the big speaking gig – he celebrated with me, for me, for us. We were a good team. Even when we traded the suburbs for the sticks, and there were times I wanted to shoot him (for giving the hens a spa day in the kitchen sink with my expensive shampoo) and he wanted to shoot me (for getting the pickup so stuck in the mud it took a tractor and a second pickup to free it), we were a good team. He farmed, I wrote farm funnies, and he read them before I shared them on my blog or included them in my books. If he laughed reading about my run-ins with rabid foxes, misguided attempts to be helpful (I believe I've told you about my unique flair for firefighting), unsurpassed talent for wrangling cattle in stilettoes, and so much more, I knew others would, too. He was a great audience and an even better editor, and I miss his handsome face.

Of course, I don't have to look too far to see it. While the boys have completely different facial structures and builds, they both look and carry themselves just like their dad. They have his sense of humor, too, and love to call or text or show up for the sole purpose of teasing me for once again finding myself surrounded by hens.

"Nice job escaping the farm, mom," Cuy says.

"It's not a farm," I reply. "We have a couple of chickens, that's all."

"Give him time, mom" Case adds. "Before you know it, Rob will have goats in the yard too."

"Goats?" Rob says suddenly. "Goats would be great!"

I glare at the two brats I've given birth to and mouth the word, "stop," but it's too late. Goats are officially under consideration.

Of course they are.

I've come to believe that there are times in our lives when God or the Universe puts us in a situation that's good for us, that we could learn and grow from, if we'd simply stop fighting it. But fight it we do, certain to the core of our being that *this* is not where we belong. I can even recall several times during my life on the farm when I stood in a field and screamed *Dear God, what did I do to have you beam me so far from my planet?*

I couldn't appreciate the lack of people, the slow pace, or the country way of dropping in during the day while I was trying to work. I was frightened of the pitch-black night, stunned by the lack of sidewalks, and crushed that a place called Cuppa Giddy Up was supposed to suffice for a Starbucks. I was a terrible cook in the land the take-out taxi forgot, a cab, subway, and car service girl who simply couldn't grasp how the horse ahead of me on the road could possibly have the right of way, and a salon-enhanced blonde who couldn't fathom trusting her hair to a place called The Mane Event.

There I was, surrounded by acres and acres of pristine pastures, at the foothills of the stunning Blue Ridge Mountains, in what others saw as peace incarnate, and all I could think was *This is so not my style.*

I was the definition of unappreciative. And immature. A flipping, flopping, freaked-out fish out of water with a smart mouth.

But God didn't give up on me.

He took my ranting and venting, bitching, and complaining, and gave it back to me as a gift that today is the thing I'm most grateful for. He gave me the gift of seeing the humor in things and a talent for helping others see it too. He gave me the gift of words, spoken and written, and the ability to use them so that others – you, I hope – can find the silver linings, the things to be grateful for, and of course the laughs in life's blackest clouds.

All these years later, my life's sort of come full circle. I'm still in the country and I'm not real happy about the hens (or the prospect of getting goats), but I've bloomed and, more importantly, bounced, where He planted me.

You can, too.

Your Daily Boost
31 quick resilience-builders

Earlier I mentioned that I keep the quote "If you can't beat fear, do it scared" taped to the wall in my office. While that one really resonates with me, there's another that means even more. I keep it framed on my desk, have a meme of it on my phone to read during the day, and I used it to open this book. It's one of the simplest yet most profound statements I have ever read, and it says, "Life is not about how fast you run, or how high you climb, but how well you bounce."

At the time I discovered that quote, I also discovered that the word bounce comes from the Latin word for resilience. Cool right? I thought so and promptly lost several hours of my life scouring Google for more information.

Almost immediately I learned three things: one, I'm a darn good bouncer; two, anyone can become a darn good bouncer, no suffering required; and three, those who learn to bounce and who build their resilience muscle, navigate, and emerge from uncertain times stronger and healthier, more optimistic, and open to new options and opportunities than those who don't.

And honestly, when aren't times uncertain? Never. So my feeling is, be ready. Work your resilience muscle every single day. A month's worth of tips on how to do that follows this note. Do them in order, jump around, it doesn't matter. Just do them.

Strengthen your resilience muscle daily and when life gets tough, you'll have what it takes to bounce back and stay back.

1
Trust Your Gut
Have you ever taken a job working for someone you knew, from the moment you sat across from them for the interview, you couldn't work for? Sure, you were probably thrilled with the salary, but I'll bet you got "Sunday stomach" six nights a week. That's no way to

live, and your gut was trying to tell you so from the get-go. Several years ago, I promised myself I'd never, ever ignore my gut again. And you know what happened? Today my gut is so good, I could lend it to people. Going on a first date? *Take my gut with you.* Job interview? *Please, bring my gut.* Considering a move to the Arctic Circle? *That's a big decision. You, my friend, may borrow my gut for a month!* The more we trust our gut the stronger it gets. If you haven't been doing so, give it a try. My gut says you'll be happy you did.

2

Do Your Thing

Every year at the holidays, when the fashion and decorating catalogs come in, I flip through them and torture myself. I look at the clothing and think to myself, "Susan, why don't you wear something more seasonal, something bright and cheery, something other than white?" I look at the decorating catalogs and think, "Susan, get in the spirit. Decorate like you did when the kids were little." Torturing myself this way gives me stress and I don't need any more stress. I'm willing to bet you don't either. So, don't do it. Do your thing and don't worry about what other people are doing.

3

Chase Your Dreams

Chasing our dreams is a risky business. It's fraught with dozens of opportunities to fail, to suffer financially, to question our sanity and the value of our pursuit. But not chasing our dreams is a far riskier business. It's fraught with sadness, depression, physical illness, and the tremendous possibility that we'll get to the end of our lives and regret that we didn't try. Who wants that? Sure, there might be people around us holding their breath waiting for us to fail, but my feeling is, they should suffocate. Chase your dreams. All you can lose is a mediocre life.

4
Go for the B
If you're like me, you give everything a hundred and ten percent. You don't just go for the A, you go for the A+. People start to know that, and soon you're getting every assignment under the sun. Sadly, some of those assignments show up at nine at night. When are they due? In the morning, of course. You're beat. You've worked all day, helped with homework, done bath time and dinner, and were looking forward to relaxing with a nice glass of wine. But you say goodnight to the family, sit down, and go for it. You give it everything your nine at night, helped with homework, bathed the kids, and handled dinner self can give. Sometime much later, you read what you've written or review what you've created and panic. It's not an A! It's B work at best! Do you stay up all night and work yourself to the point of severe exhaustion? You could. Do you wake up at 5am to try again? You could. Or you could cut yourself some slack and go for the B. Send it in. And remind yourself that only the mediocre can be at their A+ best every day – and night.

5

Get Excited!

When you've made a decision that feels right in your heart and your gut, don't give in to the temptation to second guess yourself and start worrying about all the things that could go wrong. That's putting pessimism out into the world and, when we do that, what do we get back? A bad day, a bad week, a bad month. Instead, focus on and get excited about all the things that could go right – and you'll manifest even more stuff to be excited about.

6

Super Stressed? Get Grateful

The quickest way to feel better when life or work has you super stressed is to express gratitude. Open your eyes and look, really look, for the silver lining in the "project that never ends" or the "child who never had a project he or she wouldn't wait until the last moment to tackle." The silver lining in that cloud is there. Find it, express your thanks for it, and feel the energy, peace, calm, and strength that comes when we get grateful.

7

Let It Unfold

Congratulations! You shared a dream or goal with a friend and in so doing "put it out there" into the Universe. Now, though, you're dying for something happen, for your dream to begin manifesting itself.

You're so excited, the last thing you want to hear is the word "wait." Sorry, but waiting is what you need to do. Yes, continue to put positive thoughts into the world. Continue to work toward your goal. But don't force anything. Have faith. Let it unfold.

8

You Are What You Think

I've been thinking about thinking. Specifically, I've been thinking about thinking good thoughts and how if we choose to think good thoughts and feel good, or negative thoughts and feel lousy, the amount of work is the same. So why wouldn't we opt for the positive thoughts and resultant good feelings? The thought boggles my mind. As Buddha said, "Your worst enemy cannot harm you as much as your own unguarded thoughts." Let's guard our thoughts and make sure that when we're thinking (and maybe thinking about thinking), we're thinking good stuff.

9

There Is No Control

The fact is, there are so few things over which we have control. Beyond decisions like where to live, type of career to pursue, whether to see the glass as half full or half empty – because indeed that is a choice – there are very few things over which we have real control. Control is an illusion, one that impedes resilience and results in our suffering. Better to acknowledge that reality, let go of the need to control and move forward with confidence and courage.

10

Ask

There are times when life becomes a waiting game, when the earth beneath our feet becomes as solid as a moon bounce, when nothing can happen until something happens, when we're fully, painfully aware of how little control we have over anything. It's during these times that I urge you to remember two things: One, you have control over asking for help and two, people want to help. Don't go it alone. Don't wait until you "really need it." You do really need it, and your family, friends, and community really want to give it. Ask.

11

Validation Is for Parking

The only person we should ever look to for validation is ourselves. When we look to a boss, a mentor, a significant other for validation, it's time to ask, "Why am I giving that power away?" And if you've begun thinking you're only good, successful, doing the "right" thing, etc., when someone else tells you so, it's time to extricate yourself from that relationship. Validation comes from within. It comes from knowing our worth and having faith in ourselves, our talents, our smarts, our kind hearts. When we look outside for validation, it's time to set boundaries and shore up our self-confidence. Build your internal validation muscle by staying mindful of your thoughts and actions, replacing negative self-talk with positive, and setting goals you celebrate yourself.

12

When Things Don't Work Out

So, you land your dream job and not a week into it you make some unsettling discoveries. Your boss is a micromanager. He or she is at his or her desk 24/7 and expects you to do the same. You try for a while, but it's not working out. Finally, you leave, maybe for another job, maybe to take time to regroup. When this happens, we need to ask ourselves, what did I miss? During the interview process or when I met the team, what did I miss? Sometimes there are things we didn't notice or chose to ignore. But sometimes we didn't miss anything. It just didn't work out. And that's because this isn't Hollywood. It's real life.

13

Just Take the First Step

Maybe you're thinking it's time to write that book or launch that business or that if you wait much longer to do the den, dark wood paneling will be popular again (and you can't have that). But you're worried. What if the book is awful, the business fails, or you put the house on the market only to find buyers are demanding dens with 70s paneling? We can't know how things will play out. All we can do is take the first step and have faith that the rest of the staircase is going to unfold. It is. Believe.

14

Stuck? Walk!

We've all had the experience of killing ourselves on a project with a looming deadline when bam! we hit the wall. There's not an intelligent thought left in our heads, we're exhausted, and we're not particularly pleased with our progress. Right then and there, despite the looming deadline, we need to stop and take a walk. Stroll the neighborhood or hit the treadmill, it doesn't matter. Walking loosens up ideas and triggers creative solutions.

15

Pick 3

Every day I list three things I don't want to do. For example, I don't want to finish the piece I'm working on because I'm certain it stinks, I don't want to pitch a prospective client because I'm sure they won't be interested, and I don't want to invite someone I really want to meet for coffee because I'm positive they have no interest in meeting me. Next, I make myself do all three. More often than not, I find out I was wrong. The piece doesn't stink, the prospective client wants to talk, and the coffee date is on. I don't always get three out of three. Some days I get a big, fat zero. But by pushing myself out of my comfort zone I expand my comfort zone. That's growth. And growth is good.

16

Gut Check

When your Spidey sense goes off at the same moment an opportunity you've been hoping for lands in your lap, you've got to get quiet and do a gut check. Take a pause and address what your intuition is trying to tell you. Maybe you need to heed its warning, maybe you don't. But never, ever ignore your gut. Do a gut check.

17

How To Shoot An Arrow

Have you ever shot an arrow? It's pretty simple. You pull it back, release it, and it flies forward. Life is a lot like shooting an arrow. When things aren't going the way we hoped, and we're scared and tired and worried, we feel frustrated, stymied, held back. What we need to remember in those times is that at some point, life's going to let go and launch us forward. All we need to do is hang on and have faith.

18

Just Because Your Path Is Different Doesn't Mean You're Lost

Lots of people look at me – and maybe you? – and say, "What are you doing? How will what you're doing get you to your goal?" And then they add, "I don't get it." They don't have to get it. You're the only one who has to get it. From the outside looking in, our route may seem circuitous, questionable, even crazy. Who cares? Worrying about what others think is so 2019. Have faith in your passion. Have faith in your path. Just because it's different doesn't mean you're lost.

19

Make it a Marathon

When Stu was diagnosed with cancer, a dear friend called and said, "Remember, it's not a sprint, it's a marathon." She was concerned I'd burn myself out trying to do so much so fast, and that if I didn't take our new normal at a marathon pace, I wouldn't make it to the finish line. I've thought a lot about that expression since then, and I've come to the following conclusion: The marathon pace is always the way to go. Sure, cancer is hideous and belongs in Hell. But while you're traveling that terrible journey there will still be times of levity and laughter, moments so great and loving and funny that they're burned into your memory just like any other. And if you're moving at a sprint, you'll miss them. Don't miss them. Take all of life, the highs, the lows, the laughter, the tears, the stuff that makes you say, "Did that really just happen?" (especially the stuff that makes you say, "Did that really just happen?") at the marathon pace and you won't miss a moment. Turn off your phone. Be present. Smell the roses. Slow down. It's not a sprint. It's a marathon. Enjoy it.

20

Are You Following Fake Rules?

There are rules we follow because we have to. You know, things like "pay your taxes." Then there are rules that, while they're unwritten, we still follow. Things like "don't cheat on your taxes." (This I would never do for the simple reason that I look awful in orange.) And then there are rules we make up, that live in our heads, stifle our creativity, and even protect us from – eeek! – failing. For the longest time I have wanted to create a tank top with my favorite saying on it and sell it on my website. What have I done about it? Nothing. Why?

Because real authors don't do that. For the record, no one has ever told me what real authors do or do not do. It's just a fake rule I made up and need to break. What about you? Got any fake rules that need breaking ... now?

21

No Is A Complete Sentence

So, you've set aside a block of time to work on something important. You're about to get started when a colleague pops through your office door with a cheery, "Hey! Got time for a quick meeting?" What do you say (beyond "There's no such thing as a quick meeting.")? You say no and leave it at that. Why? Three reasons. One, no is a complete sentence. Two, she or he who talks first loses. And three is tied to two: the moment you start to explain your no, is the moment you open your position up to discussion. If you have time and you want to have that quick meeting, go right ahead and keep talking. But if you don't, say no and let it hang there. Get comfortable with the silence. The first time you do it, you're gonna high-five yourself. It's utterly empowering. When you need to, don't be afraid to Go. With. No.

22

Always dress like you're going someplace better later

Want to start every day feeling like you can run the world? Get dressed. Hair, makeup, outfit, the works. Why? Remember the "Look Good, Feel Better" effort? That's why. When we look great and we *feel* like we look great, our mood improves, our confidence soars, we're more productive and effective and creative. Looking great out the outside "ups" our mental game on the inside. Always dress like you're going someplace better later because you ARE going someplace better later. You're going onward and upward, so let's look the part!

23

Rise and Rock

Great days start with great mornings. When you wake up, smile and be thankful you're on the right side of the grass. If you work out in the morning, get to it. Whatever you do in those first morning hours sets the tone for the rest of your day. When I get up, I go straight to my desk and write. After that I work out, return to my desk, and tackle whatever needs to be done. When I stick to this schedule, I have the best, most productive day. When I don't, ugh. It's not a terrible day, just not as great a day. Use your morning's wisely and win.

24

Screw the Critics

Tune out the critics. They're envious of your fearlessness. They wish they had half your moxie and guts. They have none of it. They've taken the lazy way out, sitting in their lounge chairs, sniping at your progress, success, energy, and determination. Don't be distracted by them. Remember, as Zig Ziglar said, the only taste of success some people get is to take a bite out of you.

25

Sweet Perspective

Perspective is everything. When we see a situation as dire or insurmountable, it's going to be dire and insurmountable. But if we spin it and see that same situation as a challenge, then we can figure out a way to rise above that challenge.

26

Take It at Your Own Pace

Maybe you just left your job to start your own business. Maybe you're just starting work on that fixer-upper you bought. Whatever it is, remember to take it at your own pace. It's never a good idea to measure ourselves against others who are pursuing a similar project or endeavor and who might be a bit further down the road than we are. Why? Because when we do that, it can make us feel insecure, like we're not keeping up or we're not as good as, and that's a bunch of malarkey. Whatever you're pursuing, learn from the roadblocks you encounter, learn from (but don't measure yourself against) those ahead of you on the path, share your knowledge with those starting out, and most importantly, take it all at your own pace.

27

Grief 101

When someone we love is grieving, our first inclination is to do or say something helpful. So, we rush in bearing food and hugs, and then we stand there, fumbling for the right thing to say, and then, because we're just clumsy about grief and grieving in this country, we say the exact wrong thing. Examples of the exact wrong thing include, "You'll get over it," "You'll move on," and the most egregious of all, "I know how you feel." (You don't.) There is a much kinder, gentler way to be there for someone who is grieving, and it's simply this: show up, shut up, and listen. Don't share stories about losing your Grandpa or a cherished pet; those are terrible things, but not for this moment. This is about listening to the person who is grieving. Your job is to use your ears if they want to talk and your shoulder if they want to cry. Your job is to be there and shush your hush about yourself.

28

No Doubts

When we doubt our power, when we doubt the thing we know we're great at, when we doubt what we know is the reason God put us on this planet, we give power to our doubts. The moment we ask ourselves, Why did they invite *me* to speak at that event, chair that committee, write that report? What can they possibly think *I* have to offer? we fill ourselves with nothing but negative energy. And when we do that, we exhaust ourselves, send ourselves straight down the rabbit hole sometimes for just a few minutes, but other times for a week, a month or more. Nip that negativity in the bud – and leave the rabbit holes to the rabbits.

29

Quit Qualifying

Today is a great day to stop couching our ideas in soft-sell, qualifying statements like "I'm no expert, but…" and "I'm unsure what you'll think of this, but…" With set-ups like those, the listener is already doubting our talents and capabilities. I should know. I'm a recovering qualifier. We qualify to lessen the pain of rejection. We qualify out of fear of failing. But, as Seth Godin says, if failure isn't an option, then neither is success. So, go for it. Succeed! Fail! And please, quit qualifying.

30

No More Unnecessary 'I'm Sorry's'

I used to joke that I could give a master class in apologizing for things I had no business apologizing for until I realized it wasn't funny. It was a bad habit. It made me sound insecure, and I'm not insecure. It made me sound as if I felt "less" than other people, and I don't feel less in the least. Worse still, because I was apologizing for everything, I was apologizing for nothing. If I back into my neighbor's car, you bet I'm going to say I'm sorry, but otherwise I'm working hard to pull all of those extraneous apologies out of my speech. If you're an unnecessary apologizer, I urge you to do the same. And no, I'm not sorry about it!

31

No More Playing Small

We all have talents and abilities and incredible gifts to offer the world, and why so many of us choose to hide them beneath the proverbial bush is beyond me. Our loved ones, our communities, our little corners of our Universe need us to own what we bring to the party and shine our light. This business of playing small has to stop – for ourselves and for those looking to us for permission to stop playing small too.

Made in United States
Orlando, FL
30 November 2022